New Library of Pastoral Care
GENERAL EDITOR: DEREK BLOWS

Derek Blows is the Director of the Westminster Pastoral
Foundation and a psychotherapist at University College
Hospital. He is also an honorary canon of Southwark
Cathedral.

Being There

Titles in this series include:

New Library of Pastoral Care
GENERAL EDITOR: DEREK BLOWS

BEING THERE

Pastoral Care in Time of Illness

Peter W. Speck

First published in Great Britain 1988
SPCK
Holy Trinity Church
Marylebone Road
London NW1 4DU

Second impression 1989

Acknowledgements

The extract from *The Singing Detective* by Dennis Potter
is reproduced by permission of Faber and Faber.

The poem 'Sick Child' by Anthony Thwaite (from *Poems 1953—1983*,
Secker & Warburg 1984) is reproduced by permission of the author.

The poem 'The Hospital' by Michel Quoist (from *Prayers of Life*)
is reproduced by permission of Gill and Macmillan.

The extract from the poem 'Ten types of hospital visitor'
by Charles Causley (from *The Collected Poems*) is reproduced
by permission of Macmillan.

British Library Cataloguing in Publication Data

Speck, Peter
   Being there : pastoral care in time of
   illness. — (New library of pastoral care).
   1. Church work with the sick
   I. Title   II. Series
   259'.4   BV4335

   ISBN 0-281-04325-6

Filmset by Pioneer
Printed and bound in Great Britain by
Courier International Ltd, Tiptree, Essex

Contents

Foreword

The *New Library of Pastoral Care* has been planned to meet
the needs of those people concerned with pastoral care,
whether clergy or lay, who seek to improve their knowledge
and skills in this field. Equally, it is hoped that it may prove
useful to those secular helpers who may wish to understand
the role of the pastor.

Pastoral care in every age has drawn from contemporary
secular knowledge to inform its understanding of man and
his various needs and of the ways in which these needs might
be met. Today it is perhaps the secular helping professions of
social work, counselling and psychotherapy, and community
development which have particular contributions to make to
the pastor in his work. Such knowledge does not stand still,
and a pastor would have a struggle to keep up with the
endless tide of new developments which pour out from these
and other disciplines, and to sort out which ideas and
practices might be relevant to his particular pastoral needs.
Among present-day ideas, for instance, of particular value
might be an understanding of the social context of the pastoral
task, the dynamics of the helping relationship, the attitudes
and skills as well as factual knowledge which might make for
effective pastoral intervention and, perhaps most significant
of all, the study of particular cases, whether through verbatim
reports of interviews or general case presentation. The
discovery of ways of learning from what one is doing is
becoming increasingly important.

There is always a danger that a pastor who drinks deeply
at the well of a secular discipline may lose his grasp of his
own pastoral identity and become 'just another' social worker
or counsellor. It in no way detracts from the value of these
professions to assert that the role and task of the pastor are
quite unique among the helping professions and deserve to be

clarified and strengthened rather than weakened. The theological commitment of the pastor and the appropriate use of his role will be a recurrent theme of the series. At the same time the pastor cannot afford to work in a vacuum. He needs to be able to communicate and co-operate with those helpers in other disciplines whose work may overlap, without loss of his own unique role. This in turn will mean being able to communicate with them through some understanding of their concepts and language.

Finally, there is a rich variety of styles and approaches in pastoral work within the various religious traditions. No attempt will be made to secure a uniform approach. The Library will contain the variety, and even perhaps occasional eccentricity, which such a title suggests. Some books will be more specifically theological and others more concerned with particular areas of need or practice. It is hoped that all of them will have a usefulness that will reach right across the boundaries of religious denomination.

DEREK BLOWS
Series Editor

Preface

There is a resurgence of interest in the nature of healing and of the support and care needed by people who are sick, and by those who care for them. With this growth in interest has come an uncertainty about what we mean by the term 'healing ministry', and how the Church can relate to the various places and people who engage in healing in many different ways.

This book seeks to examine some of the issues involved in the pastoral care and visitation of sick people who are being cared for within the context of orthodox medicine. It cannot be a definitive work since each pastor has to develop his/her own understanding of the meaning of any experience of illness, and of an appropriate pastoral response and style of working. Whilst it is not possible to examine every type of illness, I hope that the various situations and approaches outlined may prompt further questioning and reflection on the many different forms of illness behaviour we may meet. I believe that it is through facing questions that we are led to a recognition of both our strengths and our own vulnerability, which in turn can enable us to respond sensitively and openly to the needs of others.

The uncertainty within the Church concerning its healing ministry has been mirrored by an uncertainty within the Health Service about its own role and future. There have been several major reorganizations in recent years, a great expansion in technological and costly treatment, and limited resources to fund it all. In addition, the 'medical model' of healing, whereby the focus is more on eradicating the disease than treating the whole person, has come under critical examination. Related in part to the dissatisfaction felt in some quarters with this medical model has been the growth in alternative approaches to health care, and especially an emphasis on holistic medicine with its focus on the *person* who has the sickness rather than the sickness itself.

The broader approach to the health of the whole person is, *par excellence*, the hallmark of the Christian healing ministry. It is important that this ministry is re-established as a normal part of pastoral care, lest it become submerged amidst a variety of other approaches to healing. Pastoral care has been forced to examine its own validity and, at the same time, to examine the skills and techniques of psychology, medicine, social work, education and law, and to incorporate them *where relevant*. In many ways pastoral care is itself at a time of transition and must be clear about its function and purpose if its specific character and role in society are to be maintained. Similarly those who offer pastoral care need to be 'professional' and competent in their approach if they are to work effectively alongside other professionals engaged in health care in hospital or community. Whilst we may seek to be part of the healing team and to be seen as partners in the healing process, such a designation from other professionals is earned rather than ours by right. Although there is a great deal of 'goodwill' towards the involvement of chaplaincy and Church in the care of the sick, the onus is still on us to teach and show people that the Church has an equally valid contribution to make to the health and well-being of those designated 'sick'.

In writing this book I have greatly appreciated the advice, support and comments of patients and their families, colleagues at the Royal Free Hospital, and the many clergy and staff I have met and shared ideas with through workshops, seminars, lectures or private discussions. The best teachers are often those who have travelled through the experience and have been able to make *some* sense of it all. I hope that the text does justice to the many valuable insights that they have shared with me.

In particular I wish to acknowledge the help and support of my wife Elisabeth and my family for their tolerance and understanding of the times when I was 'Being There' rather than 'being here'. I am also very grateful to the Reverend Gwyneth Evans and Miss Gaynor Nurse for a variety of valuable advice and support. I should also like to thank the Reverend Ian Ainsworth-Smith (for permission to reproduce the list on pp. 86—8), and Canon John Browning (for permission to quote from his research), Canon Eric Reid, Deaconess Pat Atkinson, my publishers, and Mrs Hazel Clawley for preparing the index.

PETER W. SPECK
St Peter's Day, 1987

ONE

Our Experience of Illness

We forget ourselves and our destinies in health, and the chief use of temporary sickness is to remind us of these concerns. (Emerson, _Journals_, 1821)

To arrive at some understanding of what it means to be ill we should perhaps begin by recalling our own experience of some illness which necessitated a stay in bed of a few days:

The alarm rings as usual and I slowly roll out of bed. My stomach feels tense and sore and, as I stand up, I feel dizzy. The back of my throat is very sore and my eyes feel hot. Perhaps once I have had a warm drink I will feel well enough to go to work. My wife inquires, 'Are you all right?' and I reply, 'I don't know. I don't feel too good.' The thermometer appears, and my raised temperature confirms that something is amiss. 'I think you should stay put,' comments my wife, and I tend to agree—glad of the permission. Yet there are various appointments today. Am I really indispensable? I climb back into the warmth and comfort of bed and draw the duvet up to my ears.

'Why isn't Dad going to work?' drifts up the stairs. 'Because he's not well,' comes the reply. 'I wish I was not well . . . We've got double games today . . .' The noises of washing, dressing and breakfast continue. I feel distanced from the family and the house, cocooned within the bedroom and the duvet. People are already beginning to talk about me rather than to me. Their life seems to be so normal, so healthy, downstairs. My wife appears to say that she and the children are leaving. 'Is there anything else you want—another drink, some toast?' No, there is nothing. The front door closes and silence descends on the house.

I must 'phone work. I speak to the boss's secretary and

1

explain. She puts me through to the boss. 'Sorry you're unwell. Damn nuisance it has to be today with two vital meetings. Still these things happen. How long do you think you'll be off . . . Well keep warm.' I put the 'phone down. Should I get up and go in? Have I permission to stay home or not—do I need it? I turn over in the bed and hit a cold spot and quickly move back again. I feel my world has shrunk to one small warm part of this bedroom and bed. I fall into a doze.

Later . . . The family return home. Should I see a doctor? Am I well enough to go to surgery, or am I seriously ill enough to merit a home visit? I can hardly speak because of my sore throat, and my temperature has now risen to 104°. We 'phone the surgery. 'Have you any spots? Good. Then can you wrap up warm and drive over here? The doctor can see you at 6.30 p.m.' Later . . . I am pronounced 'sick' and I have tablets to take. If I am no better in a few days I have to give myself permission to be absent from work—by sending in a sick note which I have completed. If I continue to be ill the doctor will then formally give me permission to be sick and may refer me to the local hospital for further investigation. He talks about my tonsils being in a dreadful mess.

For the moment, though, I have been given permission to be ill and already I begin to feel better. Perhaps Samuel Butler was right when he wrote: 'I reckon being ill is one of the great pleasures of life, provided one is not too ill and is not obliged to work till one is better' (*The Way of All Flesh*).

Before focusing on our pastoral care to sick people it is useful to reflect on some of the factors which for us shape the experience of ill health. It is almost a convention in Britain to respond to the greeting, 'How are you?' with a phrase such as 'Fine!' or 'Very well!' even if we feel unwell at the time. So what enables us to break with the convention and clearly state, 'I feel dreadful!'? There would seem to be a process of transition from wellness to illness, with a corresponding process in reverse at the end of the sickness, of which giving permission is an important part. It is relevant to examine this process, by which we receive or desire the label 'sick', and to recognize that whilst some people accept the label readily others will vigorously resist describing themselves in such a way.

Being ill would seem to impart a status or role to the person, but one which has to be demonstrated and confirmed. In fact being defined as someone who is sick tends to separate you from other people and from normal life as part of the process to be undergone before you are allowed to adopt the 'sick role'. It was Talcott Parsons who proposed the title 'sick role' in 1951. This role, according to Parsons, has several aspects:

> Exemption from the responsibilities of normal day-to-day roles; recognition that the sick person cannot be expected to recover simply by his own unaided efforts; the sick role has its own responsibilities, since the role-player is expected to get well as soon as possible and to co-operate with the professionals. (Parsons, 1951)

The 'sick role' therefore carries with it rights and obligations. On the one hand you can claim exemption from certain responsibilities (such as work) and can claim the right to be cared for by those who are well. In addition to these rights however you have an obligation to do all that you can to get better (if possible) and to seek the advice and help of others—family, friends, general practitioner, chemist or hospital.

It is clearly routine for individuals who perceive themselves to be ill to 'consult' other lay people, to discuss symptoms, and seek advice. Scambler *et al.* (1981) asked a group of women to keep a daily health diary over a six-week period. During this time an average of eleven lay consultations were recorded for every one medical consultation. Of the 570 lay consultations recorded, 50 per cent were with husbands, 25 per cent with female friends, 10 per cent with mothers, 8 per cent with other female relatives and 7 per cent with various others (father, boyfriend, etc.). During the diary period almost all married women consulted their husbands and about half of them consulted female friends. Single women and women who were separated or divorced were most likely to consult, first their mothers, and second, female friends. The nature of the symptoms seemed to have little effect on who was consulted.

Though minor illnesses such as 'flu or cold are conditions with which we are all familiar, we tend to forget that we acquire our knowledge of these conditions and our way of coping with them through others around us. In the absence of any fellow sufferers who can impart advice and reassurance the patient can take his/her symptoms to the medical profession for interpretation. This interpretation, or diagnosis, may frequently be by successive elimination of alternative or more serious possibilities and may give the sufferer few practical recipes for coping. Some people are relieved that the uncertainty is over and they now have a 'label' to put on a certificate and to tell their friends. They have *permission* to be ill. However, people are not always helped in their search for help and reassurance, let alone meaning in the experience of illness, solely by interpretation of symptoms and the provision of a label.

Labelling and Stigmatizing

Seeking advice about symptoms needs to be seen against the background of the person's life and relationships with other people. For this reason the distinction is sometimes made between disease and 'illness behaviour', where disease is seen in terms of the actual pathology of what is going wrong with the body and 'illness behaviour' is understood in terms of the process of evaluation and action relating to our perception of symptoms.

> Illness is a feeling, an experience of unhealth which is entirely personal, interior to the person of the patient. Often it accompanies disease, but the disease may be undeclared, as in the early stages of cancer or tuberculosis or diabetes. Sometimes illness exists where no disease can be found. (Marinker, 1975)

On this basis an illness can be an indication of an impaired capacity rather than an indication of disease and should lead the physician/helper to consider interpersonal relationships and emotional difficulties in addition to any specific disease process within the body. Accuracy and competence are very important in terms of diagnosing any disease process, knowing which treatments may be appropriate, and discerning the important aspects of the patient's social, psychological and spiritual state which may influence the form and content of the help that is offered. Giving a name to what the person offers by way of symptoms is a significant part of the interaction. It is, therefore, important in diagnosing and attaching labels to consider the effect of and the desire for such labels on the person seeking help and the others involved.

Illness labels are usually only given after a period of negotiation or consultation between the doctor and the patient. Sometimes other people who are significant for the patient will be included in this process or will feature in the decision making. Some of these issues are illustrated in the story of Carol, an American, who visited her doctor in the United States.

Carol Conte was a forty-five year old, single book-keeper. For a number of years she had been both the sole support and nurse for her mother. Within the past year, her mother died and shortly thereafter her relatives began insisting that she move in with them, quit her job, work in their variety store, and nurse their mother. With Carol's vacation approaching, they have stepped up their efforts to persuade her to at least try this arrangement. Although she has long had a number of minor aches and pains, her chief complaint was a small cyst on her eyelid (diagnosis: fibroma). She related her fear that it *might* be growing or could lead to something more serious and thus she felt that she had better look into it now (the second day of her vacation) 'before it was too late'. 'Too late' for what was revealed only in a somewhat mumbled response to the question of what she expected or would like the doctor to do. From a list of possible outcomes to her examination, she responded, 'Maybe a "hospital"[ization] . . . "Rest" would be all right . . .' (and then in barely audible tone, in fact turning her head away as if she were speaking to no one at all) 'just so they [the family] would stop bothering me'. Responding to her physical concern, the examining physician acceded to her request for the removal of the fibroma, referred her for surgery, and thus removed her from the situation for the duration of her vacation. (Zola, 1973, pp. 677—89)

Carol needed the label 'sick' in order to free herself from family pressure and obligations. She had a physical symptom to present but the social factors acted as a stimulus to present herself to the doctor at this particular time. Likewise the family would have wanted Carol to be labelled as 'well' in spite of a physical symptom 'which could be attended to later' in order that she could fulfil their needs and wishes. A measure of competition of need in negotiations over labelling someone as being 'sick' may mean that people who need attention may not receive it. Carol indicates one way in which it can suit others if she were deemed to be 'well'. Similarly a mother with three young children may claim that 'I don't have time to be sick. I have to put up with all my aches and pains and just get on with things!' The family may collude with this and commend the mother for the marvellous way in which 'she keeps going'.

Some people may become symptom carriers on behalf of others who play an important part in the illness behaviour, as illustrated by John. John was thirteen and had a history of allergy, chest problems and asthma. He was attending clinic, with his mother, for an annual review of medication and routine chest X-ray and the overall picture formed by the doctor was of a quiet, pale child much younger than John's actual age who, with modern drugs, should have reached all the normal developmental milestones by this stage. The doctor decided to investigate a bit further:

DOCTOR: What sports do you play John?
MOTHER: Answer the doctor, John.
JOHN: None.
DOCTOR: Why is that John?
JOHN: (*looking at mother first*) Because of my chest.
MOTHER: Well you see with his chest and one thing and another he hasn't been able to—have you, love?
JOHN: (*mutters*) I like swimming.
MOTHER: I know you do. But you know it's not possible—especially as the school showers are so poor. You'd almost certainly catch cold and then where would you be?
DOCTOR: Perhaps you or your husband might take John. Swimming would be very good exercise for his chest and could improve his breathing.

MOTHER: Well my husband's away quite a bit—on business. We've only the one child so it's usually just John and me at home. My husband did take us swimming once but he got into a frightful temper because John took so long to change and then to dry afterwards. Proper put us off it did. You remember don't you John? (*John remained looking at the floor.*)

Further investigation showed that John's attacks were more frequent when father was at home or if mother was under stress. It also emerged that it was not a happy marriage and the mother was dreading the day when John would be old enough to leave home and she would be alone. Being classed as a 'delicate child' meant that John would need the attention and care of his mother for a much longer period and so fulfil her need to be needed. An unconscious projection of illness onto another person is not unusual where it suits the other person to have the person labelled as 'sick'. In this instance the child was acting as a barometer for the needs and tensions within the family and his 'illness' (with its very real and distressing symptoms) became the reason why various things could not happen for members of that family. Whenever any doctor, or other therapist, tried to look further into the psychosocial aspects of the illness a resistance was met leading eventually to non-attendance at clinic and subsequent transfer to another 'treatment' centre.

Some labels will have the effect of frightening the patient, and the meaning may need to be explored, since terms such as 'cancer', 'multiple sclerosis' or 'epilepsy' will have different meanings for people depending upon their understanding of the illness and their knowledge of others with the same label. A young woman who was newly diagnosed as epileptic telephoned a friend and invited her round for coffee. The friend replied that she could not come and then added, 'You see, I'd like to come, and I know you'll understand but I'm afraid of catching what you've got and I do have a family to think about. I'll give you a ring sometime.' To interpret symptoms and give a label is, of itself, not enough. The meaning and implications of the label also need to be explored and the sick person encouraged to explore the possibilities open to him/her as a way of coping and responding. Other benefits and dangers are referred to by Jacobs (1976) where he distinguishes between *labelling*, which gives the professionals power, and *naming* which leaves the control more with the patient.

> Labelling . . . runs the risk of merely giving us power, power over our clients, of telling them what is wrong, or what they are like, as well as the danger inherent in any categorisation of the loss of recognition of individuality. Naming, on the other hand, provides security to the client, not the therapist, for in the end he has to do that naming himself. It helps towards that sense of control which is based on insight and the acceptance of the less obvious parts of oneself. It recognises and explores the 'being' and the uniqueness of each individual, for ultimately it is by name that we are known, not by label. (Jacobs, 1976)

In line with Parsons' belief that the sick role carries an obligation to try to get better, the sick person also needs to be stimulated to take an active part in their own recovery. This does not always happen and the reasons are not always easy to understand, but the stigmatizing effect of some labels can be a powerful factor. Within the concept of *stigma* is the idea that all forms of illness, however caused, have the power to spoil the sufferer's social and personal identity. Some labels once they have been given seem to stick with the person long after the disease itself has been treated. Someone who has been treated for heart disease and returns to work may still be treated as an invalid with possible far-reaching effects on promotion, type of work allocated, invitations to sports activities, outings, etc. This may either arise from over-protectiveness by colleagues or out of rivalry—'I'm not sure that Colin ought to represent us at Hamburg. There is his heart condition to consider. Perhaps I had better go instead!'

Certain illnesses will be more stigmatizing in some settings than in others thus requiring a sensitivity to the patient's own cultural understanding of the illness so that any reassurance given is related to the sufferer's own frame of reference. Henley (1979) has shown that eczema, tuberculosis, asthma, epilepsy and all forms of mental illness are profoundly stigmatizing in many Asian communities in Britain. The stigma is not only for the patient but may affect the entire family. 'Some parents will not allow their child to marry into a "diseased" family. A serious disease in one child, therefore, may ruin the marriage chances of all the others.' (Henley, 1979, p.63)

Effect of Culture

If the illness is not treatable at home and we require special investigations or treatment then hospitalization is required and this will introduce us to another influence on the way in which we adopt the sick role, namely the effect of culture and of the organization of health care. The word 'culture' is here used to describe that pattern of behaviour usually accepted by the group (family, hospital, society, etc.) to be an appropriate response to the symptoms exhibited. A hospital has its own culture which can very quickly make its influence felt . . .

One morning I was making a routine visit, as the hospital chaplain, to a surgical ward. I went into one of the side rooms and met a young woman in her mid-thirties who had been admitted to the ward about three hours earlier. During that time she had been seen by a variety of people: the junior nurse who had admitted her to the ward, had recorded various details about her and put a label on her wrist; the houseman who had briefly checked she was in and had prodded her abdomen; the medical students who had come to take a history; the haemotologist who had taken some blood; the anaesthetist who had been to examine her chest prior to surgery; the physiotherapist who gave her some exercises to do; the dietitian and finally the 'big round' when the consultant came to check the abdomen and ensure that all was well for the afternoon list. It was at the end of this procession of people that I made my visit! As I entered the room I introduced myself as the hospital chaplain and said, 'I have called to see how you are settling in'. Without lowering the magazine that she was reading she lifted up her nightdress and said, 'Which bit do you want?'

In the space of just a few hours this lady had been given the very clear message that the hospital (or at least that very busy surgical ward) was concerned with 'bits' rather than people. She also recognized that the 'culture' of that particular ward was that patients should lie back and let it happen, while the experts sorted out the diseased bit of the body. By being reduced to 'bits', this lady had lost her dignity and her identity and the impact of whatever was wrong with her physically had been compounded. Responding to a situation like that is not easy and, as a chaplain, I should perhaps have replied, 'I don't want bits. I want all of you!'—but I did not think of that at the time. We were, however, able to laugh at the mistake and the embarrassment was eased. We were then able to talk about the events of that day and the uncertainty of what lay ahead of her.

It is this recognition of the temptation to focus on a diseased part rather than the illness experience which has led medical sociologists to distinguish between the words 'disease' and 'illness behaviour' as mentioned earlier. Another aspect of cultural influence, arising out of the above incident, is the way in which others may *impose their culture* and dictate the way in which the sufferer must respond or conform during the course of the illness. This may frequently occur within hospital and underlines the need to examine what patients experience at the time of admission—as shown above. Each society has a complex and interconnected pattern of language, beliefs and behaviour which enters into the very nature of illness. These must be given due weight if we are to enable the sufferer to find any meaning or understanding within a particular episode of illness. Cultural factors will, therefore, influence what we describe as illness, what we believe the cause to be, what action we should take and what are appropriate remedies. In extreme circumstances the right to be ill may be denied altogether by the prevailing culture. Thus, as Frankl (1987) illustrates, in the Nazi concentration camps those who fell ill were exterminated and the sick role was therefore replaced by the death sentence.

Chrisman (1977) studied the folk-ideas about illness in a variety of different cultures and identified four basic modes of thought about the causes of illness. He called these 'logics', and they were seen as dominant themes which permeated belief about illness, and varied in importance from one culture to another.

There was *a logic of degeneration,* in which illness is seen to follow the running down of the body—the process of ageing: 'Well what do you expect at my age?' Many people are accepting of certain chronic illnesses because they believe them to be part and parcel of getting older.

Then Chrisman described *a mechanical logic* in which illness is the outcome of blockages or damage to bodily structures. This is seen most clearly perhaps in those parts of the country where people have a strong conviction that one should have one's bowels open every day and therefore resort to purgatives and laxatives 'lest a blockage occur'! One basis for this idea is the belief that waste products will poison the system if not eliminated regularly.

Another source of illness is intrusion into the body of some foreign object. He called this *a logic of invasion* which includes germ theory and other material intrusions responsible for the illness. This is partly the result of the cultural impact of microbiological developments in medical science in the latter part of the nineteenth century, leading to the biomedical model of disease assuming almost complete dominance.

> The dominant model of disease today is biomedical, with molecular biology its basic scientific discipline. It assumes disease to be fully accounted for by deviations from the norm of measurable (somatic) variables. It leaves no room within its framework for the social, psychological and behavioural dimensions of illness. (Engel, 1977, p.196)

Here one would also wish to add 'spiritual' as defined in chapter 3.

Finally Chrisman describes *a logic of balance* in which illness follows from disruption of harmony between parts or between the individual and the environment. For example: the logic of balance is fundamental to traditional Latin American beliefs about the implication of 'hot' and 'cold' factors in illness, and is also important in classical Indian ideas of the balance between the 'humours' which determine health. Thus Harwood (1971) describes how many pregnant Puerto Rican women in New York avoid iron and vitamin supplements which they classify as 'hot' because they are thought to cause rashes and irritations (both 'hot') in their babies. Fruit juice however is 'cold'. Therefore doctors who are sensitive to the lay culture may suggest that fruit juice be taken with supplements in order that the 'cold' may neutralize the 'hot'.

The effect of labelling, culture, family interactions, hospitalization and one's own perception of the illness will influence not only the process of *becoming* ill but also the process of getting better and relinquishing the sick role. It is expected that if we are ill then we will *want* to get better, and we may meet with disapproval if we are thought to *want* to remain sick. However, there are aspects of being ill which can result in the sick person resisting any attempts to 'make them better'.

Obstacles to Recovery

1. *Resistance to getting well*

In the earlier discussion of the effect of 'labelling' reference was made to the fact that sometimes people welcome and desire a sickness label because it allows them to opt out for a while. This is a very common aspect of many illnesses, but there are other conditions which can lead to a failure to respond to treatment and contribute a powerful resistance to getting well: malingering, hypochondria and hysteria. Clear malingering seems to be rare and, whereas the malingerer deliberately imitates illness (merely pretending to be ill), hypochondriacs worry obsessively that they really are ill, so much so that they seem almost to prefer to be ill or live under the threat of it. The hysterical person can actually experience major physical symptoms such as intense pain and, in extreme cases, paralysis—all without any discernable physical fault. To the sufferer, however, the illness is *real* and no less pleasant than if the symptoms were produced by a 'real' biological disease. According to Asher (1972) one of the main explanations of this sort of behaviour is loneliness and a desire to be noticed. He implies that sometimes the 'sick role' is preferable because the person has so few rewards in life.

An example of this is an elderly gentleman who had been confined to a wheelchair for several years. He had recently been admitted into a nursing home close by a church which had an active healing ministry. He frequently attended these services, accompanied by a member of the nursing-home staff. On one occasion, following the laying on of hands, he slowly got up out of his chair and stood upright. Then he gradually took a few steps and began to walk. Some people started to talk of miracles but his nurse companion said very firmly, 'Not so, I always knew he could do it but it suited him not to.' Whatever the accuracy of her comment something had happened to that man which indicated to him that there might be more benefit in relinquishing the wheelchair than staying in it. The change in attitude and perception was possibly no less miraculous than a physical healing of an identifiable disease.

2. *Regression*

This term describes a tendency to act and think in ways that would have been more appropriate at an earlier stage of development. Usually it is not since childhood that we have been bathed, fed, cleaned and toiletted by another person or been so dependent upon others. A degree of regression and dependence may be necessary in order to allow the sick person to be looked after by others. However, the more helpless a person becomes the more regressed and dependent he or she can be, and so it is very important that sick people are encouraged to do as much as possible for themselves, as soon as is appropriate. Some people hate being dependent and will fight vigorously against it — sometimes to their own detriment.

For example, a man was admitted to a coronary care unit and told that he must rest and keep still to allow his heart to recover. If he needed anything he was *not* to get it himself but call for one of the staff. However, he was constantly jumping around the bed and seemed unable to lie still. When, on a general visit to the unit, the chaplain commented to the man about this restlessness he replied that he 'hated having to ask for everything. I'm a very independent type and want to get out of here quickly. That tracer line (the ECG monitor trace) is constantly jumping up and down and I'm trying to get into a position where it will stay flat, then I should be able to get out.' When it was *gently* explained to him that a flat line would mean that he was dead and had no heart beat, he became very still!

Sometimes people will be too independent for their own good. Others will sink, quite happily, into total dependence and be reluctant to do anything. They may become very demanding of staff and develop 'temper tantrums' if their needs are not met immediately—reminiscent of the infantile rage of the young child in respect of the mother who fails to gratify instantly the child's every demand.

People who look after the sick (carers) may be seen as a substitute parent and, as such, may be idealized as the one who will always anticipate need, be totally understanding and never let the patient down. This is not a conscious process, but it may affect the carer's responses. If the carer tries to respond to what may rapidly become unrealistic demands he/she can easily increase the natural tendency to regression and dependency. Blaming or avoiding such sick people will not alleviate the situation, since the carer has been cast in the role of 'parent' and is expected to fulfil the role of the ideal parent (through the process of *transference).* If the carer tries to respond and meet these needs (and thus reinforce this perception through *counter-transference)* the patient will go further into regression.*

Resolving situations like this can be helped by a straightforward understanding of the unconscious mental processes between carer and patient through listening, reflecting and observing behaviour. It also requires that the patient be encouraged towards as much independence as possible and the exploration of other ways of responding and coping with illness. It can also entail the sick person having to adjust to the fact that the carer is not the 'perfect' parent-figure but, in the words of Winnicott (1964), is the parent who is 'good enough' to enable recovery to take place once a healthy partnership can be established.

3. *Withdrawal*

Illness frequently encourages self-absorbtion and preoccupation with physical needs, fears, bodily functions and

* See Jacobs (1986), *The Presenting Past* for further explanation of terms and concepts such as transference and counter-transference.

medications which all lead to cocooning of oneself from the outside world (see Ainsworth-Smith and Speck, 1982, p.32, regarding 'Cone of Awareness'). The medicalization of illness often leads to people being removed from their home environment into the alien environment of the hospital, which can be experienced as segregating and fragmenting as illustrated earlier (pages 9—10). The effect of being cut off from family, friends and the ordinary and familiar things of life can disorientate and create problems when the time comes for rehabilitation or discharge from hospital. The fact that the NHS now rarely provides convalescence for patients, together with a rapid 'turn-over' rate in some busy wards, means that many people are discharged home with little time to prepare mentally for the transition. The shock of sudden discharge can lead to a rapid readmission because the person cannot adjust quickly enough, especially if they live alone. It asks a great deal of someone who has been dependent and childlike within the protected environment of the ward at 9 a.m. to be ready to move back into life as a functioning adult by 6 p.m. the same day. Some people clearly maintain a fierce independence throughout their hospitalization and are only too ready to get home but others may withdraw even more if thrust out prematurely, because they still feel 'wounded'. They may therefore cling to the sick role for much longer as a means of protection before re-engaging with life and the challenges and demands it makes of them. The presence or absence of a supportive family and friends is a key factor in how people adjust to going home or 'getting better' with the associated shift in perception from being ill to being well.

4. *The unco-operative patient*

This label is often attached to the person who is stubborn and will not accept the advice or help that is being offered by doctor, nurse, pastor or relative. This may also be associated with a lack of appreciation of help being given and can cause much irritation in the helper. There may be many causes of such behaviour ranging from lack of understanding and communication problems to a personality problem which convinces the patient that people are wanting to cause harm or upset. Another reason for refusing help is where the patient does not perceive that there is an illness to treat. This

is frequently the case with mental illness where the patient
may have little insight into their own mental state and
therefore be quite resistant to hospitalization or medication.

A further reason for labelling someone as unco-operative is
when they fail to respond in the way *we* feel they ought to
respond. 'He just will not do what I've told him to do,' or 'He's
no sense. He won't help himself at all.' Because some patients
can be very demanding and consider themselves invalids,
they can easily 'needle' those looking after them. As a result
the carer feels frustrated, tends to lose control and eventually
feels ineffective. One reason for such behaviour by a patient
can be the fact that they experience feelings and anxieties
towards staff that really belong elsewhere. Thus the feelings
expressed to a nurse, pastor or doctor may not relate to them
at all as persons, but to what they represent to the patient at
that time. This has been referred to above in relation to
regression, and it highlights the importance of those offering
care, and especially pastoral care, to have a clear understanding of their own emotional needs and reactions so that
they can more readily recognize what is happening in their
interactions with those they are caring for.

TWO

Respect for Ourselves

One can respect others only to the extent that one respects oneself.
(Sullivan, 1955)

As theological students one of our tasks on a Wednesday afternoon was to visit the local accident hospital in order to gain experience of ward visiting. The visits began in the rather dark and gloomy hospital chapel with a series of prayers. There never seemed to be sufficient time on Wednesdays to visit all the people one wished to and the rather formal beginning felt more of a nuisance than a help. However, after visiting the burns unit for several weeks and experiencing some very distressing scenes the time of preparation in the chapel changed, for me, from being a pious activity to being a vital preliminary to any patient contact. Before I could 'be with' the patients and families on the burns unit I had to attend to myself and switch off from the events of Wednesday morning in order to achieve some sense of peace within myself. Before I could attend to others I had to attend to me, and my relationship with God.

No pastor can be immune from the personal effects of a pastoral relationship. To visit, offer support and care for people in times of illness can create a mixture of feelings in the carer as well as in those cared for. People who undertake such pastoral care are usually highly motivated with a genuine desire to help others. They may be unaware of the extent to which serving others can be a way of meeting unconscious needs of their own which in turn can lead them to be quite hard on themselves as well as being troubled about whether they have done enough. Eadie (1975) has described a personality type most commonly found in the helping professions, and within the ministry in particular, which he has designated the 'helping personality'. Eadie's description

17

is based on the important work he undertook in 1972 when surveying the health of Church of Scotland ministers, and he acknowledges that his description will not fit every pastor. The two outstanding features of personality that he identified were an idealized self-image (of being loving and lovable) together with a strong sense of guilt leading to self-criticism and self-denigration. Because of the image that a pastor feels must be portrayed any 'unacceptable' aspects of personality will be hidden but can emerge indirectly in relation to others and, therefore, have the potential to distort the pastoral relationship.

> For instance, his own guilt and ideal expectations may be unconsciously projected on to others stimulating feelings of inadequacy, guilt and anxiety. Or, in satisfying his own need to help, he may unwittingly encourage dependence, helplessness, and passivity. Moreover, if he cannot accept his own sexuality or aggression, he will be inclined to suppress and neutralise such impulses in others. (Eadie, 1975, p.12)

Working with people who are ill or hurt will necessarily induce stress in those offering support, in addition to those outlined above, and this should be anticipated. Each pastor should seek to identify his or her own areas of vulnerability and the stresses to which they are most susceptible — whether these originate from within or without the person. Such reflection and insight can allow the person to monitor themselves sensibly and take any necessary common-sense steps to maintain a good balance. Such examination is not only necessary for our own mental health but also to enable us to maintain a good involvement with others. Eadie sees a need, therefore, for training in self-awareness and self-development as a necessary ingredient of ministerial training. He also believes that pastors must examine any reluctance to utilize available help when they need assistance for themselves. Sufficient attention must be given to 'recreation and personal satisfaction which are so necessary if he is to gain relief from tension. Personal needs for satisfaction and fulfilment are usually sacrificed in the interests of vocational duties. In consequence, the minister's marriage, family life, social interests and leisure may all suffer.' (Eadie, 1975, p. 14)

Sullivan (1955) expresses this in terms of 'respect' when stating that respect of oneself, through paying attention to our own needs and stresses, is a fundamental prerequisite to respecting other people and being able to care for them. Hence the focus at this point in the text on the pastor *before* proceeding to look at other aspects of the pastoral care of sick people. In New Testament terms it is the aspect of our Lord's command which is often ignored—'Love your neighbour *as yourself*'—which implies a proper love of self, a respect of self, which can then free one to love one's neighbour (Matt. 19.19).

Boundaries in Pastoral Care

An important part of respecting oneself is recognizing the necessity of setting limits or boundaries within pastoral relationships. There are a wide variety of boundaries relating to such things as confidentiality, time, degree of involvement, frequency of meeting, personal beliefs, and the amount of our own life experience that we may share with the other person. Recognizing that there are boundaries is one thing, actually managing them successfully is another.

For example, we may advocate that relaxation and leisure are vital aspects of a healthy life style. If we find, however, that our own personal lives are diminishing and that we have no time to pursue the sort of recreational activities we recommend to others, then the balance is wrong and our personal boundary has been breached. We may, in mitigation, entertain the fantasy that 'things will slow down'. However, it is more likely that demands will increase in proportion to our effectiveness to help and so the opportunity for change and rest may decrease. If we can acknowledge that natural breaks will *not* arise, then we may be more able to take responsibility for creating our own breaks, without feeling guilty. Caring should not become equated with martyrdom. A lack of respect for our own bodies, needs, and personal life can so easily lead to our taking on too much, becoming exhausted and then finding that our effectiveness has diminished.

Alternatively, we may find ourselves tempted subconsciously to use the helping relationship to satisfy needs of our own which are not appropriately met within the pastoral relationship. Because it is not always easy to identify that this is happening for oneself it can be helpful to have an individual or group outside of the situation to whom one can go to discuss such issues and gain more insight into what we are doing and why. Having a supervisor may be one way of meeting this need.

Areas of Vulnerability

A surprising number of people have been 'put off' hospital visiting as a result of being sent to 'do the hospital on Friday afternoons' with little preparation or opportunity to share the feelings of inadequacy and distress which such visiting can create. This can result in our feeling less confident about how we shall cope with whatever may happen during the visit and enhance any feelings of inadequacy and vulnerability. If we believe that being vulnerable is a sign of weakness not of strength we may fail to see it as an important growth point. In addition it may clash with our own internal (idealized) image of the invulnerable, all coping, pastor who may then defensively avoid sick-visiting lest his vulnerability be exposed.

We all have areas of vulnerability which often relate to unresolved needs and conflicts in our personal life and which can become more apparent to us as we relate to people who are sick or dying. The things most likely to trip us up in any pastoral situation are those relating to aspects of our own lives which we have failed to attend to. This is seen very clearly in terminal care and bereavement, where those offering support need some awareness of any unresolved grief arising out of previous experiences of loss. The prospect of personal death is an uncomfortable one for most people and is usually only contemplated when circumstances force us to do so. Our attitude towards life, death and life after death will influence the way in which we relate to the dying and the family, since entering into a close relationship will raise *our* anxieties and bring us face to face with the fact that one day we will die. If this is an unpleasant and anxious thought it can lead to our avoiding dying people and developing strategies to defend ourselves from becoming involved. The fact that clergy preach and teach the resurrection life does not necessarily mean that they have no anxieties about their own death. In fact they may feel the pressure of expectations that they will have no problems about this 'area of expertise' which can make it hard to admit to very human fears concerning the act of dying if not of death itself. It can help if we are able to do some work on our feelings about mortality, and whether or not we see death as a failure, together with some understanding of our own expectations of ourselves.

One way of looking at this is to create a personal life-line along which one marks off all the losses (the significant and the seemingly insignificant) which we can recall. Then to select the most significant loss and try to recall the *feelings* that we experienced at the time and subsequent to the loss occurring. It is best if this exercise is undertaken with someone else so that the feelings can be shared, even if the nature of the loss itself is not revealed. The feelings generated by such an exercise are an indication of the unresolved work relating to that loss. It is important to recognize these and what they belong to, since it is these same feelings which can become exposed as we related to others in the crisis of their own loss, or impending loss. To create and examine a personal life-line in this way can be painful for some people, but the control of personal emotions lies not in turning away and denying them, but in facing them so that we can recognize, understand, and live at peace with them.

Developing a personal philosophy of life which can help us in *our own* search for meaning in the situations we share with people who are ill is also an important part of coming to terms with our own vulnerability. This may be achieved through attending to our own spiritual life and growth as well as meeting with others with whom we can discuss and share issues relating to spirituality, health, suffering and pain. Side by side with a grasp of the psychological understanding of human behaviour in illness should be the spiritual development of the pastor lest the central focus of *pastoral* care be lost. (See further in chapter 5.)

Loneliness can contribute to the vulnerability of many who exercise a pastoral ministry, and the onus is usually on the pastor to arrange his or her own support network. Because of the isolated way in which some clergy work, the effects on the pastor of short-term relationships with sick people within a hospital may be more marked. Brief, intense, crisis work can be very stressful, especially if one does not see any results or progress from the amount of energy and effort put in. Because it is difficult to measure effectiveness in many situations, it can raise issues of self-worth and value for the pastor. This process was demonstrated many years ago in the report on the health of Scottish clergymen which stated that 'Fears about personal failings and inadequacies, together with sensitivity to criticism and opposition, are predominant in the anxieties of these clergymen' (Eadie, 1973, p.29). Similarly, in recent articles relating to the personal life and personality of the pastor, both Foskett (1987) and Eadie (1987) refer to the inner conflicts which the pastor may experience as a direct result of pastoral care and which will need to be attended to if he/she is to be able to continue to care effectively. Many of these conflicts focus on expectations which may be unrealistic and therefore stress-provoking when it is realised that one cannot live up to such high ideals.

If there is no one person or group to share these feelings with, the sense of isolation and futility can grow and lead to more feverish activity in an attempt to prove one's usefulness. Within a hospital community there should be several people around who can be approached for support, either formally or informally, and it should be easier to make appropriate referrals of difficult patients and families. Within the community the pastor needs to discover the various resources available which he or she can use personally, as well as on behalf of the sick person, and so relieve the pressure of feeling that 'It's all down to me'. However, the problems of isolation and lack of appropriate feedback as to one's value and worth are not unique to the clergy, since they are also experienced by community nurses working solo on the district and by single-handed general practitioners and others. Some of the possible remedies for this situation are equally applicable to others involved in health care and can sometimes be approached on a multi-disciplinary basis. (See chapter 10.)

Continuing Education

Those caring pastorally for the sick should involve themselves in continuing education, whether in the form of private reading, attending seminars, group meetings or conferences. Such opportunities may be provided by the local Health Authority or the Church. A local branch of the Guild of Health, the Guild of St Raphael, the Churches' Council for Health and Healing or the Insitutute of Religion and Medicine will have meetings as well as magazines where issues of this nature can be discussed or read about. For those concerned with hospital chaplaincy (whether whole-time or part-time) the Hospital Chaplains' Fellowship has branches in many parts of the country and, as an *ecumenical* fellowship, it offers a forum for training, support and fellowship in a variety of ways. It also produces a magazine which is written by and for chaplains and, therefore, is an invaluable source of current thinking and reflection on pastoral care within the Health Service. The Training Officer of the Hospital Chaplaincies Council (a Council of the General Synod of the Church of England) also arranges training courses of varying lengths and depth in different parts of the country. (See Appendix A for details of these various organizations.) In-service training may, therefore, meet a variety of needs (personal and professional) including an update of knowledge, the practising of new skills, the enhancement of self-confidence and understanding, together with fellowship and support from others involved in a variety of forms of pastoral care.

Supervision

Supervision can cover a variety of activities ranging from the industrial context of maintaining standards within the institution to the pastoral context of ongoing training and development with a more experienced pastor or with someone at the same level as oneself (peer-group support/supervision). Within supervision a relationship is formed of trust and acceptance which can enable the pastor to share and explore anxieties, inadequacies and mistakes and thus grow in that experience. The relationship with a supervisor can mirror or reflect the relationship between the pastor and the client and lead to greater understanding, self-awareness and growth. As a pastor one needs to learn how to assist the patient in discovering meaning in the experience of illness and to find solutions to his/her problems which are not damaging or more disabling. Whilst one can read about such processes and gain much in this way, it is not always possible to properly appreciate and understand the underlying signals and messages expressed by patients in indirect ways without experiencing such processes ourselves in relationship with someone else, i.e. the supervisor. Supervision will not always be couched in psycho-dynamic terms, since many solutions can be the result of applying common-sense to the problem as a result of sharing it with someone else. For example, if we find that we are overloading ourselves emotionally, it may be the result of how we have structured our day in that there is little variety in the nature of the tasks we undertake. Reviewing our diary to ensure that we don't lumber from one emotionally draining activity to the next throughout the day may relieve some of the overloading.

Conclusion

It is with the human experience of sickness, and the search for meaning within it, that those offering pastoral care should be most concerned. In seeking to minister to the sick we are concerned to share with the other person their experience of becoming ill, being ill, and the hope of recovering from that illness, whether the person is at home or in hospital. In the course of this sharing we would also hope to make known God's continuing love and power to transform our experience of suffering, and to declare him to be the ultimate answer to our quest for meaning. This desire is expressed in the ancient prayer-book collect now included in the rite of anointing within the Church of England:

> The almighty Lord, who is a strong tower to all who put their trust in him, be now and evermore your defence, and make you believe and trust that the only name under heaven given for health and salvation is the name of our Lord Jesus Christ.

The way in which we might achieve this aim will vary greatly from person to person, and we shall need to remember that whilst sickness might make one more open to consider the ultimate issues it also makes us more vulnerable. Therefore we need to beware the danger of abusing the opportunity of access to sick people, and of 'cashing in' on the captive audience! The people we care for will not expect us to be *perfect* pastors (parents) provided that we can, to use Winnicott's term, be *good enough* pastors (parents) in respect of that person in that situation. Awareness of our own needs and ensuring that we attend to them in an appropriate way will enable us to respect and respond to the *person* who is ill as they search for meaning in that experience. In order to appreciate the spiritual nature of that search it is important to distinguish between religious and spiritual needs. In the next chapter the distinction between the two terms 'religious' and 'spiritual' and the central part they play in our ministry to sick people will be explored.

THREE

Distinguishing Needs —
Spiritual and Religious

A bodily disease, which we look upon as whole and entire within itself, may after all, be but a symptom of some ailment in the spiritual part. (Nathaniel Hawthorn, *The Scarlet Letter*, 1850)

At 11 p.m. one Saturday evening the sister-in-charge of the intensive therapy unit telephoned the local vicar, who was the chaplain 'on-call' that night, and asked him to come to the unit. A teenage girl had been admitted in a critical condition and her father had asked to see 'the hospital vicar'. On arrival at the hospital the vicar went into the unit to find out what was happening and to gain some impression of the girl's condition. The sister explained that the girl had skidded on the road, come off her moped and gone under a lorry. She had severe brain damage and the outlook was very poor. She said that the parents were in the waiting room and had asked to see somebody from the Church.

When the chaplain entered the waiting room he was greeted by the girl's father who thanked him very much for coming at such a late hour. The only other person in the room was the girl's mother who sat in a corner by the window and seemed quite oblivious to all that was happening. The father stood in the middle of the room and so the chaplain also remained standing. The girl's father then asked the chaplain whether he knew what was happening, to which the chaplain replied, 'Only a brief outline. Perhaps you could tell me?'

The father explained that his daughter Claire had come off her scooter, been hit by a lorry and was very ill. He implied that the lorry driver had not been looking as he approached the junction.

'I'll be honest with you, Vicar,' he said, 'I don't go to church often but I've always lived a decent life, as she'll tell you' —

26

indicating his wife who sat looking into space—'I also teach swimming to kids and, over the years, I've saved a few lives. Well . . . I reckon this time God owes *me* a life. You're a vicar, and you're going to get it for me. I need a miracle, so get down on your knees—AND DO IT NOW!'

There was no doubting the menace in his voice and he was now standing between the chaplain and the door. The chaplain therefore sat down, thinking that he was a big chap and it was probably wiser and less threatening to take a lower position. The chaplain decided not to challenge the father's statement but to acknowledge the seeming unfairness of what had happened. However, in his own mind he had also decided that it was not appropriate to comply with the father's order to say a series of prayers and perhaps leave—at least not yet.

The father's anger became more open and his hands were made into tight fists. The chaplain said, 'I feel that you are very angry with me, and what I represent.'

'You're dead right. Why should this happen to us? Claire had everything she wanted. I'd do anything for that girl. Why doesn't he take my life instead—answer me that. You're the man with the collar round your neck!'

Feeling all the uselessness and the pain that the father had put onto him, the chaplain said, 'At the moment I don't understand why this has happened, but I think we have to face the fact that your daughter may die.'

At this the father started to storm around the room kicking the chairs and the table and saying how useless and ineffective vicars were when you needed help. Eventually he sank on his knees in the middle of the room and began to hit the floor with his fists, crying, 'I want a miracle, I want a miracle.'

At this point the chaplain joined him crouched on the floor (head to head, with his hand on his shoulder) and, after a while, again asked the father to tell him about his daughter, what sort of girl was she, what had happened that day. Gradually and painfully the story emerged.

Earlier that day the father had bought his daughter a moped. He brought the bike home at lunchtime and gave it to his delighted daughter. He showed her where the brakes were and the throttle, and how to start it. Then she set off for her first ride up the road. At the end of the road the surface was greasy and she skidded out of the side road and into the path of a passing lorry.

Then her father said, 'It's my fault, I've killed Claire, the only one I've really loved. Why doesn't God take me?'

The chaplain could see that much of the anger against God was arising from the father's guilt and sense of responsibility which was too painful to face. Therefore, it was all projected against God (or in this case against the chaplain who represented him). Now that this was more openly acknowledged it became possible for the chaplain to talk about forgiveness and reconciliation. He was also able to state that he believed God to be a God of love who does *not* abandon us in such situations but can give healing and strength to us when we are suffering. The strength and healing, however, may be the strength to face the fact that their daughter might die—that healing might come through her death. Therefore it was important to face things honestly and, if need be, to say goodbye to their daughter properly. The chaplain was also very aware of the physical and emotional distance between the husband and wife (as expressed in the comment, 'I've killed Claire, the only one I've ever loved'). It was clear that if the father was to find peace he would need help to accept *his* portion of the responsibility, though not all of it, and to be reconciled with his wife and with God.

At this point the chaplain said, 'Before we put this whole situation before God and pray about all that we have shared together, and your hopes and fears for your daughter, I want to try and include your wife in what we are doing.' Eventually the chaplain was able to reach the point where the husband and wife were able to go with him into the unit and to pray with him by their daughter's bedside. The next morning the medical team decided that Claire showed no signs of brain activity, declared her to have 'brain-stem death' and that there was no purpose in continuing ventilation, unless the parents needed more time to come to terms with what had happened. Later that morning the chaplain was informed that Claire had just died and that both parents would like him to be with them, when they went to see her to say goodbye, and to pray with them.

Just as the medical profession may be tempted to focus on the disease rather than the broader experience of the illness, so those offering pastoral care may be tempted to focus on the clearly expressed *religious* needs (symptoms) and miss the less obvious *spiritual* search that may be taking place. The initial meeting between the father and chaplain began with a clearly stated *religious* request—'I need a miracle, so get down on your knees . . .' The chaplain might have responded to this request by accepting it at face value, saying some prayers (and perhaps anointing the girl) and then going home having promised to visit again. It can be very tempting to get out of a sticky situation by promising to visit again, as commented on by Nahum Tate (*Dido and Aeneas*, Act III):

> Take the bowsey short leave of your nymphs on the shore,
>   And silence their mourning
>   With vows of returning,
> Though never intending to visit them more.

Such unfulfilled promises can lead to a variety of problems in hospital or parish, as instanced by the difficulties experienced by staff within a psychiatric or geriatric unit when an elderly person is 'deposited' there by relatives who promise to visit but have never done so; or the clergyman who promises to visit (when notified of someone's illness, or following a funeral) and fails to do so. He will find his relationship with that parishioner very strained if they do eventually meet.

The hospital chaplain or local minister may well find it easier to respond to clear requests for sacramental or other religious ministry, especially when they find that this fits very neatly into the culture of a hospital ward, or when it allows them to protect themselves in a threatening situation (see Wilson, 1971). If, however, we are focusing at the wrong level (religious need/somatic symptoms) we may well miss the underlying *search for meaning* which the sufferer is wanting to share and explore if only the right sort of relationship can be formed.

It appeared initially that the father, in the above situation, was seeking a miracle to restore his daughter to what she had been before the accident. Had this understandable request been granted he may never have needed to acknowledge his part in the whole incident and thus could have avoided facing the guilt that he was feeling. It is quite common in situations like this for people to want to 'turn the clock back' as a means of avoiding the consequences of an action; and to seek some religious ritual which will magically put things right. It was important in this instance for the chaplain to give the father opportunity, or space, to ventilate his feelings and to show him ('model' for him) that God still loves and cares for us when we are angry with him. The fact that the chaplain didn't assume that it was only a religious need allowed the relationship to develop (albeit painfully) so that the underlying search for meaning and the need for reconciliation could be identified. It was at this point that a religious response could be made which would be more meaningful because it had grown out of the relationship they had established.

In addition to distinguishing between the religious and spiritual needs of people, a further distinction may be drawn between 'wants' and 'needs'. What we want is usually an expression of a wish, whereas needs are more closely related to basic human requirements. Someone who is sick clearly *wants* a complete cure, a miracle, or relief from symptoms. It may, as in the situation described earlier, be the relative who expresses the 'want'. At the same time the person may *need* support in coming to terms with the illness, any treatment which is necessary, and their own reactions to it. There is also the need to be understood as a person who, come what may, will not be abandoned or deserted because of what they have done, the feelings they may express, or the nature of their illness.

It is, therefore, pastorally helpful to distinguish between the *spiritual* and the *religious* needs of people in times of sickness or distress.

Spiritual relates to a concern with ultimate issues and is often seen as a search for meaning, and echoes Frankl (1987 edn) who has said, 'Man is not destroyed by suffering, he is destroyed by suffering without meaning.'

The spiritual issues may be expressed in questions such as, 'Why should this happen to me? Why now? What have I done to deserve this—it doesn't seem fair . . .' These questions are more spiritual than medical and may be directed at anyone who is nearby. When a person is trying to find some meaning within a particular experience they will look in many different directions, starting with the things which have helped them make sense in the past. It may be that the person has developed a philosophy of life which has always been able to give them the answers they searched for, and thus enabled them to cope. This philosophical approach may have had nothing to do with religion—in either its folk or its orthodox form. Others may express a belief in God which has never found expression and practice within an orthodox religion, but to which they look to 'bring me through'. The arrival of a clergyman may be seen as a God-given opportunity to vent one's wrath or to seek answers to these questions. The questions (and the ambivalence they may reflect) may not be expressed if the right relationship of trust has not been developed since 'one should always be polite to vicars'.

Religious relates more to the need to put into practice one's usual expression of spirituality. This may be expressed as the need to see a priest, to attend chapel, have time to meditate, receive the sacraments, etc.

It is much easier at the time of admission to elicit *religious* rather than *spiritual* needs by the asking of questions. The 'nursing process' is a method of caring for and relating to the patient which encourages a greater degree of personal involvement, so that the patient is more clearly recognized as a person. At the time of admission a nurse will elicit the patient's physical, emotional, social and spiritual needs and then plan an appropriate pattern of care to meet those needs. Although the nursing process is designed to avoid a 'cross-examination' approach, by creating a relationship with the person, it can be misused as a questionnaire. When this happens the patient may be asked, 'What is your religion? Do you wish to see a chaplain? Any special requests?' Asked as straight questions these will usually elicit needs relating to religious practice rather than anxieties and concern with ultimate issues. Staff may, however, be under the impression that what they have recorded and acted upon are the *spiritual* needs of the patient. Once these needs have been elicited, staff may then send the chaplain in to 'do his stuff', whilst they get on with theirs. This can restrict the chaplain's role to that of a dispenser of religious goodies which can be done without forming a relationship or entering into any real dialogue. This approach and conception of the chaplain's role can be easier for hospital staff in that the priest does not get in the way and they can more clearly define when he is needed. It is also easier for the priest who is feeling threatened by the sick or the dying to hide behind the ritual and use it in a defensive manner.

Each month a clergyman would take communion to a 60-year-old lady, who was confined to a wheelchair with arthritis. She always had everything ready for his arrival and he would enter the flat with the words: 'Peace be to this house,' continue with the service, and then end by saying, 'Do remember, underneath are the everlasting arms' — and leave! After several months of this she could stand it no longer. When the minister referred to the 'everlasting arms' she exploded and said, 'They're no damn good to me. They won't get me out of this chair to do the things I want to!' Somewhat red-faced, the clergyman sat down, apologized, and said, 'I'm sorry. I never realized, but I've always used those words at the end of house communions.' 'Well, that's as maybe,' she replied with a smile, 'but I just want you to know I can't stand platitudes — they don't help me.'

From that point on the two of them met as people and got on very well together. The relationship had moved from meeting a specific religious need to acknowledging the wider needs of the *whole person*. An element of mutuality had entered into the relationship and, as time went by, the clergyman learned something of the frustrations of handicap and the spiritual distress experienced by this lady.

Good pastoral care is concerned with the way in which we can discern and hold together the religious and the spiritual. From the chaplain's point of view it will also mean that he/she may share some of the pastoral work with others who have related to the sick person and who have been invited by that person to join in their search for meaning.*

A priority for the clergyman, therefore, is the creation of a relationship of trust which allows for the expression of

---

* cf. Campbell, 1981, ch.7, and the concept of the pastor as a 'companion'.

feelings and fears. This may best be developed through an openness on *our* part with attention being paid to the *assumptions* about appropriate behaviour and responses we may hold; the *value* of an experience to that person whose experience it is; and ensuring that we create *opportunities* or *space* for that person to share their experience with us — if *they* wish to. For example: if we meet someone who has experienced a traumatic loss and is clearly quite distressed we might say, 'I know just how you feel'. In fact there is no way in which we can know *just* how anyone else feels, since only they know what their reactions are. Only they know the value of what they have lost and we cannot establish trust if we act on assumptions without testing those assumptions by providing the opportunity for the person to share their feelings with us. By not imposing our own reactions onto them, and not suggesting to them how they *should* be feeling and reacting, we are closer to the genuineness of concern which is so important. It is this genuine interest that enables the person in trouble to share in an open way knowing that we will allow them to express whatever they wish in their own way.

In addition to attending to the above we shall also find it beneficial to develop basic relationship skills — such as listening; attending; responding — as described in the work of Egan (1982) and Jacobs (1985). Once the relationship has been established the sick person may then provide various indications of *spiritual* distress:

1. *Sense of meaninglessness/hopelessness*

This may be expressed as frequent cynical comments about treatment or the people offering care. The sick person may see little point in continuing treatment: 'I'd be better off dead than living like this.' The person may become apathetic or withdrawn, as typified by the request from a nurse to a chaplain, 'Please come and see Alice — she's turned her face to the wall.'

2. *Intense suffering*

Intense suffering exacerbates the sense of hopelessness. 'I can't endure this anymore; where's the sense in going on like this?' Pain following an operation and leading to healing is different in quality to the pain experienced by certain secondary growths of cancer. Purposeful pain is more endurable than pain for which one can see no purpose. Intense suffering encompasses many things in addition to pain, such as loneliness, isolation, vulnerability—all reminiscent of the 'dark night of the soul' and the threat of non-being. Requests to 'end it all' are both an expression of spiritual distress and a challenge to the care being given—'If this is the best you can do, I'd rather be dead.'

3. *Remoteness of God, inability to trust: break with religious/cultural ties*

Statements that one no longer believes in God, that God is dead or lets one down, are often accompanied by a feeling of powerlessness and emptiness inside. When people break with their culture or religious practice, this cuts them off from a wide variety of ways of coping with crisis. The reasons for this may be that their life philosophy does not answer the questions being raised by the illness, or that their view of God is that of a young child and now seems irrelevant to what is happening in adult life. Such situations may cause great feelings of insecurity and may be expressed as an inability to trust the people who are trying to help. 'How can I trust man if even God has let me down.'

4. *Anger towards God, religion, clergy*

If the sick person feels let down by God or some divine power it is not surprising that some anger should be felt towards those who represent that power. Defending God is something that those exercising pastoral care can easily be drawn into, since a full-frontal attack on what we value and hold to be true can lead us to defend God—even though he does not need defending—because *we* need the reassurance.

Alternatively the person may seek to placate this divine power with especially good behaviour: for example, 'I will show people how believers cope with illness. I won't let God down'—the stoical approach.

5. *Sense of guilt or shame*

There are many people who feel that whatever illness they

suffer from it is a result of some wrong doing in the past. If they can put that right, then perhaps the illness will go away. This may be expressed in statements such as, 'I don't deserve to get better'.

Sometimes illness can fulfil a purpose for the person who is sick in that it can be a form of escapism or a way of keeping someone in a dependent relationship. 'You know that if you make me cross by not doing what I say you could give me a heart attack!' Behind this statement there may also be a measure of guilt and understanding that the illness is being used in a manipulative way. Acknowledgement of this can be painful because it would lead to exposure.

Some treatments and surgical procedures can have the effect of radically altering the appearance of the person, so that they feel unacceptable to other people and stigmatized by the illness. This may result in feelings of shame over a colostomy, a skin complaint, or loss of hair following chemotherapy, leading to comments such as 'Who would want me like this?' If you also lose your control over bodily functions and thereby your dignity, then your sense of shame can be heightened. The ministry of reconciliation, forgiveness, and loving acceptance can be of great importance in such situations, because they speak to the deep anxiety that if I and other people cannot accept and love me as I now am, then surely God cannot love me either. It is a short step from here to a feeling of utter desolation and spiritual distress.

6. *Concern with moral/ethical nature of treatment*

This is exemplified by the sick person who frantically searches for advice on what decisions to make: 'Do *you* think I should have this operation?' or 'Why spend all this money on me, at my age? I've had my life—they should spend the money on some young person.' Such feelings of unworthiness may relate to guilt and shame (see 5 above). The inability to decide may simply be because the person has always been indecisive, but it may be an indication that they are afraid to die and so must make the right (life-saving) decision— whatever the final quality of life may be. This may be related to the phenomenon of bargaining in terminal illness where the dying person seeks 'just a bit more time, please' (see Kübler-Ross, 1970, chapter 5). However, the person may still seek the approval of others (not least God) that what they desire is morally acceptable.

7. Unresolved feelings about death

When visiting the sick it can be helpful to inquire what sort of night the person had—did they sleep all right, did they dream? Fears of going to sleep and therefore resisting sleep are not uncommon in sick people who are afraid that they might die. The longer you stay awake the longer you stall death. Disturbing dreams and a preoccupation with death, or a morbid humour, are also indications of unresolved feelings concerning personal death. Serious illness, even if not life-threatening at the time, still 'concentrates the mind wonderfully' and raises questions regarding what is beyond death—or letting go into what?

This is the fundamental ultimate issue for pastoral care to address with all the implications it has for hope and understanding about life after death and, in Christian terms, what incorporation into the Body of Christ means for us. In addition to reassurance the sick person may well benefit from sacramental ministry—whether in the form of Holy Communion, the ministry of healing, or (if at the point of death) the viaticum.

These spiritual needs may be discerned by the chaplain/ pastor or others caring for the sick. Our response to them may be in the form of sharing their pain, bewilderment and doubts, and creating a safe space in which some of these things can be shared. How one responds to the various needs which sick people and their families express will depend upon the people concerned. It is clear that there will be as many styles of pastoral care as there are people practising it. However, one should usually establish a relationship first and then decide what form of ministry is appropriate (if any) as that relationship develops. Failure to do this can lead to imposing a religious ritual on to a person at an inappropriate time or in a way which does not match the spiritual needs of that person—if they were allowed to express them. Clearly there will be occasions, especially during a crisis or emergency, when there will be little opportunity to form a relationship, since the prime need is to 'go in and get on with it'. Nevertheless it would seem important, even in these crisis situations, to spend even a few minutes gathering the salient facts about what has happened and making some assessment of the spiritual state of the patient and family before opening one's pocket manual.

Sometimes, therefore, our response *will be* in the form of a specific religious ministry which will be all the more meaningful, where opportunity allows, for having arisen out of a relationship which enables the prayers, etc., to reflect something of the spiritual quest which has been shared together.

FOUR

God's Resources for Health

───────

Those who are called to minister to the sick have the duty of setting free all of God's resources for health. (Archbishop of Canterbury's Commission, 1958)

These words from the report of the Archbishop's commission of thirty years ago are as pertinent now as they were then. Whilst medical science in its various forms is capable of diagnosing and treating a wide variety of diseases and conditions, there are some resources for health that it does not possess. Within the Christian tradition these resources belong properly to the Church, especially as it exercises its ministry of healing, usually in close harmony with the medical and surgical approach and care.

Unless one is exercising a specific ministry to sick people, as in hospital chaplaincy, it is usual to be visiting people whom one knows and who now are sick. This means that usually one has some knowledge of the person being visited and of their views and possible wishes about ministry on such occasions. However, such knowledge needs to be checked with the person *before* we proceed to minister religiously, since the timing and the setting may prove to be wrong, or we may not be responding appropriately to the needs at that time, leading to embarrassment rather than comfort!

God's resources for healing are made available to the sick in many different ways and especially in the context of a loving and caring community. This implies that there needs to be a harmonious relationship and partnership between Church and hospital which may be expressed through the presence of a duly appointed chaplain and/or through the wider Christian presence within the staff and patients of the hospital/community. It is important to note the represen-

38

tational aspect of sick-visiting whether at home or in hospital, in that the visitor represents not only their own concern for the sick person but also that of the local church which they have come from, and Christ himself as present within the Church and sacraments and thus present in the context of the meeting. 'Truly, I say to you, as you did it to one of the least of these my brethren, you did it to me' (Matt. 25.40). (For further discussion of this aspect of visiting see chapters 5 and 6, and Wilson (1983).) Thus there is a divine context to each visitation even if this is not always made explicit, and this chapter therefore focuses on the more explicit religious response to the spiritual needs expressed and shared.

Prayer and Bible Reading

An essential part of maintaining any relationship is communication and this is equally so in the realm of spirituality. Thus the sensitive use of scriptural passages and prayer with and for the sick are very important resources for healing. We may be thinking of the prayer offered individually and privately by the sick person, or it may be prayer offered in the home or by the hospital-bedside with the sick person. Alternatively it may be in the context of a prayer group meeting regularly to pray for all sick people within a particular place or community. 'I don't go to church much, Vicar,' said one lady, 'but knowing there's a lot of people out there praying for me has kept me going.' Many people whom one meets in hospital ministry bear testimony to the tremendous support they receive from knowing that they are being remembered and prayed for in many and various places. 'Do you know,' said the same lady, 'they've even got Catholics praying for me!' There are many people who pray regularly but because of their illness or pain find that at present they can no longer pray in the way they usually would. This can cause distress, especially if it means that they cannot maintain their usual rule of life whilst ill. One young lady, who had been hospitalized several times, said, 'If I've been ill I have always found the greatest cause of emotional distress was that when you really want to and need to pray you're too tired or in pain. It's as if a resource that you take for granted is whipped away just when you need it most. There seems to be an assumption that your faith will sustain you, but often it doesn't without some sort of help.'

In that the essence of prayer is focusing upon God it can be helpful pastorally to suggest some simple acts of recollection/ meditation such as, 'Be still and know that I am God'. Short acts of affirmation which help the person to focus on God first and their own condition second can often be beneficial. These statements may be given verbally or may be printed on prayer cards or leaflets. It is more helpful if such cards utilize clear type-faces and a size of lettering which enables them to be read by elderly people, as well as by patients lying down following a 'pre-med' injection prior to going for an operation and therefore experiencing difficulty in focusing! Design and choice of prayer cards is a very individual thing, but in selecting prayers or statements to be printed one should reflect on what one might be saying theologically about the patient's condition and God's possible response. This is especially true in relation to some of the tracts which patients produce for you to read which have been sent by a well-meaning friend and which may reflect a very punitive understanding of sickness.

One of the problems which frequently accompanies sickness is that of losing control over many aspects of your life and body. This can leave some sick people with a strong feeling of uselessness. Joyce had a muscle-wasting disease which over a period of years led to her being paralysed from the neck downwards. She longed for a way in which she might contribute something instead of always receiving. She was in her late sixties when I first met her and had been prepared for Confirmation by my predecessor in the chaplaincy. She explained to me that the chaplain used to visit her and give her the first names only of some people he wished her to pray for. She would then include these people in her own prayers and found that this had helped her to feel a contributor again. She continued to do this until she died four years later. There are many sick people who might contribute, and themselves be helped, in this way. However, the patient who believes that God has sent him or her into hospital to fulfil a mission while they are there, and therefore goes round all the other patients fervently praying for them, presents a different problem for the chaplain!

If, as mentioned earlier, prayer is focusing upon God, then offering up our situation in openness and using our own words is also of importance. As we pray to God 'unto whom all hearts are open, all desires known, and from whom no secrets are hid . . .', we may then be more able to express to God any puzzlement, anger, resentment or despondency we may have and not feel that we must always be polite to God—because he knows all about it already!

One question which frequently crops up in training sessions and discussions is 'to pray or not to pray'. There cannot be a hard and fast rule of never or always since this must arise out of a sensitive response to the needs at the time. To always pray may mean that one imposes on a 'captive' audience who may not like to say stop. Never to pray may leave some people feeling disappointed and let down. It should arise naturally out of the meeting and not be forced. In some instances it may suffice to say that you will remember somebody at the Eucharist or at a prayer group meeting. Others may appreciate a period of silence while you both focus on God in your own way, perhaps followed by a blessing. Some may wish you to offer to God the substance of what has been shared in the visit—not necessarily in a set prayer but reflecting some of the anxieties and the thanksgiving that were expressed. Prayer at the bedside should usually be short, unobtrusive and as natural as possible. There is usually no need to change posture; continue as in normal conversation with the sick person, perhaps holding their hand at the time.

In respect of biblical material it should be the sick person who sets the pace and whose wishes are paramount. Many patients will wish to have a particular version of the Scripture because they cannot cope with new and unfamiliar things at such a time. The gospels and the psalms are a rich source of strength, as are the various anthologies and treasuries of devotion which one can obtain. From the point of view of pastoral care it is really a matter of flexibility and trying to find what is of help to this particular sick person. This is especially so for hospital chaplains who may find themselves ministering to people from backgrounds very different to their own, and of other faiths than their own. (For further discussion of this area of ministry see *Our Ministry and*

Other Faiths, 1983.)

In many cases people may not be able to cope with words in any form but may derive great support from a simple small wooden cross that can be held in the palm of the hand. To quote Toplady's hymn Rock of Ages, 'Nothing in my hand I bring, simply to thy Cross I cling'. Alternatively an icon or some other religious picture or symbol may serve as a suitable focus for devotion.

C.S. Lewis once said, 'I am, often, I believe, praying for others when I should be doing things for them. It's much easier to pray for a bore than to go and see him.' To pray for the sick must include some preparedness to be used as part of the answer to that prayer either directly or indirectly. Thus a prayer group for the sick should perhaps be involved in some way with visitation so that in their intercession they can reflect some of the pain and difficulty of those they meet. Whether or not the intercessions are a part of the normal worship of the church or a smaller group meeting in the home to pray for the sick, the focus should be the person not the medical details. Otherwise there is a tendency to focus on the problem and not the person. Similarly intercessions which are too generalized ('We pray for those sick of this parish' or 'those sick in our midst') may enable people to avoid any active response and thus forget St Augustine's maxim: 'Without God, we cannot. Without us, God will not.' Frank Wright in his very helpful and reflective book writes:

> In praying for the sick, it is surely sufficient to name individuals followed by periods of silence. Where prayer-groups exist, it is easier for them to do this in their meetings than in the course of public worship, and many prayer groups do this very well. When they specifically meet 'to pray for the sick', there is always the danger that they focus exclusively on 'sickness', and become morbidly centred on it. I have noticed that good and well-intentioned individuals can come to love passing on 'bad news' about other people's illnesses — and this danger exists, multiplied, in a group unless great care is taken to focus positively on God, his love, and his wish to heal. (Wright, 1985, p.56)

Sacramental Resources

In discovering and sharing the spiritual needs of sick people it may well emerge that the appropriate response should be sacramental. I have written elsewhere in this series of the sacramental response in relation to death and dying, much of which is equally relevant here (Ainsworth-Smith and Speck 1982, p.68f.). For example, baptism in the hospital setting tends to be in response to an emergency and at a time when the baby's life is in danger. Marriage is only arranged when one partner is too ill to be moved from hospital and is unlikely to recover from the present illness. Other sacraments are clearly relevant in times of sickness and appropriate to other situations than terminal care. Where such ministry is undertaken in a hospital there should be good liaison with the ward staff *and with the hospital chaplain* where one has been appointed.

Holy Communion

This is the supreme act of thanksgiving and healing in which the communicant, through the body and blood of Christ, receives grace and strength in a unique way to sustain them in whatever they have to face. Whether the administration is at home or in hospital it is usual for the service to be abbreviated, not least because concentration is not good when you are unwell. It is useful to use a service leaflet or card containing the main parts of the service, preferably in clear typescript. This can be left with the sick person, especially if it also contains some devotional material. Many clergy have a regular list of 'house communions' which they go to on, say, a monthly basis. Many of these people will have been receiving communion in this way for a long time and a routine will have established itself — possibly including coffee and biscuits afterwards! The clergyman may bring the sacrament with him from the church where it was consecrated or he may consecrate the bread and wine as part of the service in the home. He may be on his own with the sick person, there may be members of the family present, or members of the congregation. The presence of others can clearly help the sick person feel that the community/congregation is supporting and caring.

In the case of communion in hospital it may not be so easy

to arrange a congregation. However, by liaison with the staff it may be possible to group together one or more patients who wish for communion. It may also be possible to arrange the communion for a time when the family or others are visiting—if they wish this. Again one should not assume that this is what the patient or family will necessarily want. It is usual, in hospital, to use a pyx to take communion to patients. This may be a single pyx in which one places the consecrated host/wafer which may or may not be intincted with wine. Alternatively one may use a double pyx which also contains wine so that you can intinct the wafer with wine at the time of administration. Some patients in hospital may wish for communion before an operation and may be 'nil by mouth' from midnight. Much depends on the time and nature of their operation, but it may be possible to give them a fragment of intincted wafer on the day of the operation if they are not going to the theatre until a few hours afterwards, or one could give communion the night before and avoid any anxiety about receiving immediately prior to anaesthetic. Some patients find swallowing a wafer difficult and a small drink of water can help. This is especially true with patients who have had a stroke or who have illnesses such as myaesthenia where the throat muscles may be weakened.

Immediately after an operation a person may still be 'nil by mouth' or have a tube passed through the nose and down the throat (naso-gastric tube). In such circumstances it may be difficult to receive a wafer but it may be possible to receive in one kind by receiving wine on a spoon. If the patient is anxious about this it may be better to advise an act of spiritual communion or to administer the laying on of hands and anointing instead. Sometimes the patient will be in isolation because of an infection or because their treatment has lowered their resistance and they are likely to pick up any infection that others may be carrying—and priests, like doctors, are not 100 per cent sterile! Such patients are usually 'barrier nursed' which means that one must wear a gown, gloves and sometimes a face mask before entering the room. Anything which is taken into the room has to be left there or has to be sterilised first. Rather than decline to take Communion to such patients it is possible to obtain a small sterile pot from the ward staff. The consecrated host/wafer can then be placed into this pot prior to the 'communion round' and then taken in to the patient and the pot left in the room afterwards. In all cases of barrier nursing clergy should liaise closely with ward staff to avoid increasing risk for themselves or the patient. Whilst receiving communion is not the only way in which we can receive God's grace, nevertheless for a great many people it is of such importance that we need to be fairly flexible in the way in which we administer in order that those desirous to receive may do so. Having said this, one will still meet people who will decline communion when it is suggested on the grounds that 'I will wait until I am better'. This may reflect a rigid understanding that one should only receive in church and at an 8 a.m. service, and that sitting in bed in a nightie is not a seemly way to meet the risen Lord.

Laying on of Hands and Anointing.

The feelings of alienation and isolation that some people experience when they are ill can sometimes be relieved by physical contact. Some years ago I was visiting a patient in an Intensive Therapy Unit (ITU). She had been commended to me by a local parish priest who told me that she was a regular worshipper who was recovering from a major operation. I spoke to the staff who gave me some background information about the patient and the operation and then I went across the unit to see her. She was unable to speak because of the tubes in her mouth which connected her to a breathing machine (ventilator). However, she was awake and I could see in her eyes that she was terrified. I put out my hand to take hold of hers to find that it was seized in a vice-like grip which said very clearly, 'Don't go'. I sat by the bedside for nearly an hour, neither of us saying very much as I watched my fingers going blue! While I sat there the nursing staff came across several times and I slowly realized that none of them actually touched Janet. They spoke to her, explained what they were doing, but then stroked and emptied the catheter, took the blood pressure, checked the drip, the blood transfusion and the ventilator but never actually touched or held her. When eventually Janet let go of my hand, indicating that she wished to sleep and that I could leave, I talked about my observation to the staff—while I massaged my hand. They were a very competent and caring group of nurses but they admitted that they had not been aware of the lack of physical contact nor the patient's need for such reassuring touch.

This experience may service to illustrate the dual benefits of the laying on of hands. There is the clearly religious aspect of blessing and peace which is conveyed by the imposition of hands by the priest and perhaps others who may be present. There is also the fact that, for many people, being held and touched has in itself a healing and restorative property, especially at times when they are feeling isolated or depersonalized in some way. Coupled with this is the importance of having someone with you who can *be* with you as opposed to *doing* things to you. Many of the people one meets in the course of visiting the sick may not have been held or had physical contact with another person during that day (or week). There is, perhaps, relevance in thinking about the 'ministry of touch' as distinct from what can be a more formal laying on of hands. Clearly one is not thinking in terms of sexual contact in this context, but there must be times when it is appropriate to give someone a hug because this will be the most therapeutic thing to do.

To some extent this is cultural, in that some groups have no such taboos about touching, but the same issues may arise in respect of touch as were discussed earlier in relation to prayer. 'At what point, if at all, should I pray (make contact with) this distressed person?' As with prayer it is not advisable to intend to touch everyone or no one, but to be sensitive to the needs and wishes of that individual. Much will depend on the situation and circumstances but we should perhaps reflect on the nature of any anxiety we may have in respect of physical contact with sick people.

The more formal laying on of hands can be seen as a very normal action of the whole church, being exercised through the minister, bringing an expression of loving care to the person who is ill. This corporate aspect is made clearer when others are present and serves to illustrate the commitment of the church to stay with the sick person and continue to care whatever the outcome. Whilst this ministry may be exercised in the local church, in the context of the Eucharist or special healing service, it may easily be administered at home or in hospital. The involvement of others in this ministry helps to overcome a natural temptation towards attraction to the healer rather than focusing on the love of God present in the sacrament.

Whilst the laying on of hands may be regularly administered, the sacrament of anointing is normally only administered once during a particular episode of an illness. The oil used is ordinary pure olive oil which has been blessed either by the Bishop on Maundy Thursday, or by the priest himself prior to or as part of the service. The Second Vatican Council sought to restore this sacrament to the wider ministry of healing instead of restricting its use to times of extremis. This sacrament is normally restricted to baptized members who understand and use the sacramental life of the Church. It is generally reserved for those who are seriously ill but not necessarily dying, sick persons who are experiencing great suffering or pain or whose condition is deteriorating. Children as well as adults may be anointed. As with the laying on of hands, so with anointing, others should be present to represent the wider group involved in the care of that person. It is also important to spend time preparing the sick person, and those who will be present, as to the meaning of the sacrament in order to guard against magical interpretations.

Joan and Anne, two teachers in their early twenties, were involved in a car accident. Both were admitted to hospital where Joan was found to have a broken leg whilst Anne had a fractured collar bone and a potentially serious head injury. They worshipped regularly at a church local to the hospital and their own vicar visited both women and liaised with the chaplain about their care. Joan made a good recovery and visited Anne on a neighbouring ward. Anne could not speak, but could hear, and Joan expressed concern that she was clearly very frightened. Since she could not receive communion, Joan asked whether Anne could be anointed. This was explained to Anne who nodded her assent and a time was arranged when the hospital chaplain, local vicar, Joan, a friend from church and the ward sister could all be there. Over the weeks that followed Anne made a slow but good recovery. When she was able to talk more easily about her experience she described the time when she was anointed. She said that it was like nothing else she had ever experienced.

At the time of anointing she felt that there was a large ball of orange light at the foot of the bed which glowed and gave off a warmth which went right through her. 'It was so powerful', she said, 'that I don't think I would want to receive that too often. However, I was very frightened before that time but afterwards I felt a great sense of peace. I knew within myself that I was going to be all right.' This experience of powerfulness leading to a deep sense of peace is quite common with anointing, and although people may express it in many different ways it frequently leads to a transforming of attitude and approach.

The restoration of the sacrament of anointing to a more central place in the ministry of healing could lead to misunderstanding and charges of irrelevance or magic if it is divorced from the practice of orthodox medicine. Michael Wilson drew attention to this danger many years ago when he wrote:

> The restoration of such a sacrament to everyday use in the Church today will accomplish little unless it is symbolic of, and accompanied by, a very much deeper insight into the sacramental nature of all created things, including those things which God has given man the power to make. 'For the earth is the Lord's and everything in it', not only natural herbs but manufactured penicillin . . . If it is desirable for a Bishop to bless oil for healing purposes on Maundy Thursday, is it not equally desirable for him to visit the hospital dispensary and operating theatre on St Luke's Day, to bless the medicines and surgical instruments which God has given man the power to create? But would such blessing be any better understood than the blessing of olive oil is understood, unless it was a visible part of the Church's awareness of the living God at work in the hospital today? . . . somehow penicillin, scalpel and hypodermic syringe must be gathered within the ministry of Christ's hand stretched out to heal. (Wilson, 1966, p.40)

Wilson's comments serve to illustrate the importance now, as then, of a collaborative approach between the Church and medicine in the work of healing.

Confession or the Ministry of Reconciliation

In defining 'spiritual' needs (chapter 3) it was suggested that these relate to the search for meaning within a particular experience. Irrespective of its nature a time of sickness provides an opportunity to reflect not only on the meaning but also on some of the 'if only's' that many of us have in our lives. To some extent we can live with these regrets but there can come a point when we need to attempt to put them right or make amends. Lying in bed at 2 a.m. when you are unwell and unable to sleep is a common time for people to dwell on such episodes. Sometimes people are able to sort out these areas of their lives for themselves, once the 'if only' has come into focus, but others may need help.

A very important part of hospital chaplaincy, and of the healing ministry, is that of reconciliation — towards God, other people, ourselves, or past memories. The way in which this is undertaken will vary from an informal sharing of the need to 'put the record straight' to a more formal 'purple stole' act of confession followed by a formal pronouncement of absolution. Whilst an act of confession is an integral part of all the healing sacraments there are times when it needs to relate to very specific things in the person's life. It is not always easy to hear a confession in a hospital ward. Clergy will be familiar with the way in which all conversation around the ward seems to stop when the patient says, 'I confess . . .' It is often easier to have privacy in the older style 'nightingale' wards than in a modern four-bedded room where there is little to distract the attention of other patients. It may be possible to take the patient to an adjacent office, or the hospital chapel. If the patient is bedfast it may be possible (without too much fuss) to move the patient's bed to the treatment room on the ward for the short time required.

An important part of any act of confession is an appropriate act of thanksgiving for the state of grace into which it brings the penitent. One criticism of certain healing services is that they seem to dwell too much on our being 'miserable sinners' and so do not give sufficient emphasis to the redemptive love of Christ and his power to heal and save.

A deep sense of guilt can certainly sap the energy of a person and retard the progress back to health that they might otherwise make. This is especially true in relation to people who find themselves 'bound' by past hurts or memories. Pastoral counselling and the appropriate use of an act of confession can do much to enable the sick person to let go of the past and free them to live more fully now. It is important here to discern a pathological sense of guilt (and the compulsive confessor) which one may encounter in ministering to the mentally ill. Absolution and spiritual counsel can bring great comfort to the emotionally disturbed but there should be, as far as possible, a close liaison between chaplains/clergy and those providing psychiatric care for the patient. It is often possible to liaise well without in any way breaching confidentiality or the 'seal of the confessional'. It can also be very reassuring to the sick person to see that the Church, medicine and psychiatry are not necessarily in opposition or competition with each other. This is especially true for those patients who see reliance on medication as a sign of lack of faith in God and therefore a further source of guilt.

Corporate Acts of Worship

Hospital chapel or day room

The facilities available for corporate worship vary enormously from hospital to hospital, and within the wide variety of community residences for sick or elderly people. The *Hospital Chaplaincies Handbook* provides information about what hospitals should provide by way of space and equipment, but it is usually left to the chaplains to decide what use is made of such provisions. It would be wrong (even foolish) to be too definitive about this but many patients clearly benefit from being able to get out of the ward area and meet together for a corporate act of worship which is neither too lengthy nor so formal in its structure that patients begin to feel embarrassed about attending in nightwear!

The magazine *Hospital Chaplain** has contained several articles over the years describing the patterns of worship which have been evolved by the chaplains in a variety of different hospitals. In some cases it is possible to have a high

* Published by the Hospital Chaplains' Fellowship—see Appendix A.

degree of congregational participation, as for example in some units for mentally handicapped people. In other cases there might be good ecumenical sharing which allows a variety of different forms of worship and co-operation. Whatever the pattern or place for worship, decisions about timing, transport of patients, and any necessary permission for staff to attend whilst on duty should be worked out between the chaplaincy and the appropriate departmental managers. Non-Christian groups may also wish for facilities for worship and may look to the chaplains to support them in either sharing facilities already available or in helping them find some suitable alternative. For example, in one hospital Muslim staff members use the chapel vestry for their prayer times so that they can have privacy together with facilities to wash and perform the necessary ablutions. To make inter-faith use easier it is helpful if the furnishings of the chapel, and viewing rooms attached to mortuaries, are easily removable to allow for use by other groups (see *Our Ministry and Other Faiths,* 1983).

In some hospitals it is feasible to broadcast the services from the chapel to the wards via the hospital radio link. This can be a mixed blessing, especially if it is a live broadcast from the chapel! Problems with the equipment may cause headaches in that headsets may not work, the radio may not be switched over, patients may have difficulty finding the channel on the radio or it may be necessary to stop the service because a patient has been taken ill in the chapel. These difficulties are not insurmountable, but it may be easier, where there is a hospital radio, to use pre-recorded material either in the form of a talk, a meditation or a pre-recorded act of worship. Broadcasting to an unseen congregation can be disconcerting, especially if one is broadcasting from the hospital radio studio. The pre-recording of special services in the chapel or local church, such as a carol service, an Easter Mass, or a Passover service may be much easier to organize. It is possible for clergy and others to attend courses arranged by the BBC in order to gain some of the skills necessary for broadcasting on local, national or hospital radio networks. (Details can be obtained from the Hospital Chaplaincies Council — see Appendix A.)

Ward services

In some hospitals there is no chapel and any corporate
worship has to take place in the ward itself or in the dayroom.
Creating the right atmosphere is a very important part of
such services and, whilst the arrangement of the room needs
careful thought, the use of appropriate music can be of great
benefit (see Raggett 1986). To some extent 'ward services'
have become a thing of the past for many chaplains in
hospitals. Some would curl up with embarrassment to think
of the way years ago a group would march into an orthopaedic
ward (albeit by arrangement with the staff), switch off the
television and announce to the captive audience that 'we are
now going to have a service'. To 'take over' a ward and inflict
worship on to people is to invite confrontation and resentment
as depicted so graphically by Potter in *The Singing Detective*:

> *Coming through the double doors into the ward is a sudden
> surge of newcomers. About eight or nine people, in
> 'ordinary' clothes, though they are all on the hospital staff,
> either as nurses or junior doctors or auxiliaries. Something
> about the glow on their faces, and the way they stride, even
> their haircuts, and the manner of their dress indicates
> what they are: Evangelists. Not just Christians, but eagerly
> buttonholing, chapel-orientated, what-think-ye-of-Christ,
> good-cheer, good-news fanatics. One of them has a case,
> which looks as though it holds some kind of instrument.
> An earnest girl starts going from bed to bed, handing out
> hymn sheets, with an insistent smile.*

> GIRL EVANGELIST: Please take one. You'll be able to
> follow the words. (*And on—*) Please take one. You'll be
> able to follow the words. (*And on—*) Please take one.
> You'll be able to follow. Please take one!
> *But some are too weak or too far gone to respond.
> Meanwhile, the others have clustered in the centre of the
> ward. Dr Finlay, a houseman in his worldly life, begins to
> address everyone.*
> DR FINLAY: If I could have your kind attention, please.
> Everyone. *Good* afternoon! My name is Dr Finlay. And
> may the Lord Jesus Christ be with you!
> *Marlow's eyes roll in incredulity and disdain.*

MARLOW: Oh, no-o-o!

The earnest girl tries to hand out a hymn sheet to the next bed she has reached, that of the nod-nod-nodding old man.

GIRL EVANGELIST: (*Quieter now*) Please take one. You'll be able to follow the words—

Nod-nod-nod.

Or perhaps you'd prefer just to listen—

Nod-nod-nod. She withdraws

Yes. Well. Jesus loves you.

DR FINLAY: Let me introduce ourselves to you. (*Simper*) If introductions are necessary. We, all of us, we all work here in this hospital, as doctors, as nurses, administrators, or whatever. And we, who have ourselves experienced the direct and personal love of our Saviour, the Lord Jesus Christ, wish to share this love, this grace, this *joy* with you, today, on the Sabbath Day—

GIRL EVANGELIST: (*To Marlow*) Please take one. You'll be able to follow the words

MARLOW: (*Loudly*) No.

GIRL EVANGELIST: (*Startled*) It's a hymn sheet, and—

MARLOW: (*Violently*) Stuff it!

Hearing the one and only objection, Dr Finlay momentarily falters—

DR FINLAY: We—ah—We ask you only that—Yes. Today, this afternoon, we go from ward to ward, to invite you to share with us the infinite joy and comfort we have ourselves received—

MARLOW: (*Loudly*) Leave us alone! Why don't you bugger off and leave us in peace, Finlay.

(Potter, 1986, pp. 152—3)

Such situations are often best avoided by ensuring that contact is made with the various patients before any act of worship is arranged. A confrontation of the sort described by Potter is invited by the use of 'steam roller' tactics, when even the most vulnerable can find the energy to object if pushed to do so. It may be easier to arrange for a service in a dayroom so that only those who wish to worship can be brought by the staff. If the ward itself is to be used the willingness of the patients (whose space it is) should be sought and suitable arrangements made for those who do not wish to participate (for example, by their going into the dayroom, TV room or far end of the ward). Because of the multi-cultural and multi-faith aspect of many of our wards the imposition of a particular religious service could give additional offence to those of other beliefs.

However, there are still many areas where ward services *may* be appropriate when *sensitively* undertaken. These services may be a communion service/mass or a non-denominational 'songs of praise' structure. All that has been said earlier about captive audiences and powerful evangelism are as applicable to a dayroom service as to ward services. The use of a good-quality cassette player is essential, together with pre-recorded hymns which are singable. Suitable music before and after the service can also help to settle people down and put them in the right frame of mind for worship. The choice of hymns and other material used in the service will be dictated by the type of congregation expected and thus will vary greatly—from the geriatric ward, to the mental handicap unit or the maternity department. Length of services is an important consideration, since many sick people find it hard to concentrate for long. People may find it physically difficult to sit for long, either because of stitches or arthritis or the need to go to the toilet. In that many people do not like to draw attention to themselves they may feel embarrassed about walking out of a service, or standing up and walking around, and therefore may suffer in silence and decide never to come to a service again. Apart from keeping such services reasonably short (i.e. approximately half an hour) some statement at the beginning about informality and permission to leave if necessary can help people to feel more at ease and able to focus on why they are there.

Funeral and memorial services

Within the life of any institution the occasion will arise when a member of staff or a long-stay patient will die. It is not always easy for an institution to find an expression for its grief, and the local church or chaplaincy may be able to respond to the need for an appropriate expression of feeling by arranging a memorial service. Sometimes these can be very clearly Christian in format and expression, but sometimes they may need to be broader in expression. For example, if the humanist Professor of Medicine dies after thirty years' service to the medical school and hospital there may be a secular funeral in keeping with the views of the deceased. However, this may be followed by a memorial service expressive of the views of the family and staff, many of whom may be non-religious or of a non-Christian faith. Such services should include participation by colleagues, and the address may be given by the appropriate colleague, friend or departmental manager. A memorial service merits careful preparation since it can enable the chaplain or minister to 'speak' to the institution and facilitate grieving.

In a similar way it may be appropriate to arrange a service following the death of a long-stay resident to enable the other residents of a unit, ward, or home to have an opportunity to say their own 'goodbyes'. Some may be able to attend the funeral itself if, for example, a minibus is available to take them. It may sometimes fall to the chaplain or local minister who attends a long-stay unit to suggest or arrange for this to happen. In some mentally-handicapped persons' units the residents will have been together for many years and so will have formed very strong relationships. The death of one of their friends or 'family' can produce a very marked grief reaction which may be helped by an appropriate outlet such as the funeral.

Because of the DHSS provision for hospitals to arrange for the funeral for stillborn babies, or neo-natal deaths, it may be that parents do not attend the funeral of their child and subsequently experience difficulty with their grieving. This could be addressed through a suitable service in the chapel or local church which enabled the parents to 'let go' of their child and say their goodbyes properly. There is also a growing number of people who are delivered of a child prior to twenty-eight weeks' gestation and for whom there is no legal requirement or provision for burial. The report of the Royal College of Obstetricians and Gynaecologists (RCOG) has rightly recognized that some of those parents wish to know what happens to their baby and to arrange for a burial or cremation. This is especially so if the child is between 20 and 28 weeks gestation. Such an arrangement is usually made privately with the funeral director, local minister or hospital chaplain who may be asked to help. The obstetrician and gynaecologist will need to provide a letter stating: 'I HEREBY CERTIFY, that I have examined the non-viable fetus of . . . . delivered on . . . . which was less than twenty-eight weeks gestation and has shown no signs of life' (RCOG, 1985, p. 1).

When the child's body is donated to the hospital for genetic investigation a service could be held in the hospital chapel/local church, with or without the baby being present. If the baby's body is present then a suitable small white coffin should be obtained into which the baby can be placed, both for viewing (if appropriate) and for the service itself. After the service the baby can then be returned to the histopathology department for the ensuing investigation. It is usual for pre-28-week babies to be classed as 'fetal material' and therefore to be 'cremated' within the hospital after all the investigations are complete. It may be possible to arrange for the separate 'cremation' of the fetus in question so that the ashes (small in quantity) can be retained for subsequent burial. A local church may be willing to allocate a portion of its churchyard for the internment of such ashes. This can bring great comfort to many women who for years afterwards may otherwise wonder 'What happened to my baby?' with associated feelings of guilt and abandonment.

Where services of the kind described above are arranged by a hospital chaplain, it is important that there should be some liaison, if possible, with the appropriate clergyman in the community who may be able to continue the pastoral care begun in the hospital or maternity unit. In the case of a part-time chaplain these two roles may coincide. One way of enabling the link between the whole-time chaplain and the local clergyman to become real for the parents may be if they can both be present for the funeral/memorial service in the hospital chapel or local church. Where parents do not wish to be put in touch with a clergyman in their own area they should be offered the opportunity to return to the hospital to see the chaplain they have related to there, or given information of support groups such as SANDS or the Miscarriage Association (see Appendix A). Unresolved grief can seriously affect relationships for many parents and especially their feelings about any subsequent pregnancy.

The manner in which we are enabled to 'let go' of someone who has died is a crucial part of this process, and the above services may do a great deal in conveying God's continuing loving care at a painful time in their life.

Clearly there will be other opportunities for pastoral contact with staff through corporate acts of worship such as a service of thanksgiving at St Luke's-tide for the work of the hospital, the Christmas Carol Service, or at the time of the closure of a hospital unit. The beginning and the end of nurse training may be other opportunities for a religious, as well as a secular, rite of passage. Such occasions are all means of helping to build up a sense of belonging and of community. Thus they may help to mitigate the isolating effect of some aspects of institutional life and, therefore, speak to some of the spiritual needs of the institution which people might otherwise find hard to express.

Healing services

The title 'healing services' conveys a variety of different messages to people, and it is important to be clear in our minds what the term means for us before we arrange services with such a title in our own pastorate. Strictly speaking all services which proclaim the Word of God, where the Sacraments are administered and received in faith, are healing services whereby people may be restored and God's power and glory proclaimed. In this sense baptism and Holy Communion are great healing events, and the Church is exercising a healing ministry every time it meets to worship and glorify God whatever the form of that worship. Whilst many would want to argue that the right and proper context for the ministry of healing is within the communion service, nevertheless there may still be a place for a service which enables people of other traditions to participate more fully in the entire service.

There are now many resources available as guidelines as to how such special healing services might be constructed. These range from the rites produced by the Church of England, the Church in Wales, the Roman Catholic Church, and those produced by the St Marylebone Parish Church (Hamel-Cooke, 1986), the Guild of St Raphael (see Appendix A), to the variety of services one might encounter within the more charismatic religious groups. Whilst there may be many who offer healing outside of the Christian tradition what is clear within Christianity is that healing comes from God and we are the instruments through which God's healing power is conveyed to those in need. Because of the variety of different understandings and expectations of healing services it is important, as Hamel-Cooke (op.cit.) describes, to ensure that the expectations of those attending are addressed. It is also important that if there is to be anointing and the laying on of hands the distinction between these should be made clear (see pp. 45—8 above), usually in the address which should be part of the ministry of the Word. Because of the emotional content of such services every effort should be made not to exploit the emotions of those present but to establish a sense of peace through the words and the silences, the readings, music and hymns that are chosen. Since many of the people who attend such services are vulnerable, care should be taken not imply a spiritual blackmail in the sense that 'if your faith was stronger you would have been healed'. In many cases the disease process or disability may be unchanged, but the inner attitude to the illness may be changed as a result of attending healing services—perhaps over quite a long period of time. *We don't heal, God heals* and this can best be demonstrated by those who will administer the laying on of hands themselves receiving healing before others come forward to receive. This corporateness is an important way of saying that God is healing *in and through* the whole Church and helps to prevent one individual person being identified as 'the healer', thus drawing people away from God.

Others have written more extensively on the nature of healing and concepts of health and wholeness (e.g. Wright, 1985: Wilson, 1975), but what is fundamental to all who have written about the Christian healing ministry is the need for a good rapport and co-operation between the Church, the family, the sick person and those offering orthodox medical care. In wrestling for an understanding of suffering and pain we perhaps need to explore every possible agency of healing, and for each agency to recognize its limitations. This is part of the uncomfortable relationship at present between orthodox and alternative medicine. The Churches' Council for Health and Healing has proposed a voluntary code of conduct for all involved in a healing ministry (CCHH, 1986). This helpful document provides sensible guidelines for those who minister to sick people at home or in hospital and refers to the DHSS directive on healing organizations which states:

> It is for the patient to indicate that he wishes to be visited: that is the first consideration. It is then for the health authority to exercise its discretion as to permitting the visit with due regard to the views of the doctor in charge of the case. This latter consideration has more particular reference to the psychiatric patients. (DHSS, 13 July 1978)

The health authority would invariably consult with the chaplaincy in the event of such a request before exercising its discretion. In our pastoral care if we can be discerning, and strive to maintain a spirit of co-operation between those involved with the person who is sick, we shall then be able to fulfil our 'duty of setting free all God's resources for health' (Archbishop's Commission, 1958).

FIVE

Aspects of Visiting

―――――

Just then Mother, Mary and Jim, Mary's husband, came in. Jim walked purposefully up to the bed and immediately handed me everything he had in the way of conversation. He said, 'You look fine.' The rest of the two hours he spent looking longingly out of the window or examining me from different angles, as if I were a building site . . . they were so curious about everything in the institution and I was so curious about everything at home that the two hours were up almost at once. Just before they left Jim said, 'Very little is known about tuberculosis. How is the food here?' I said it was wonderful and he said, 'Well that's something'.
(MacDonald, 1962, p.75)

Visiting sick people is a very important activity because it bridges the gap between the sick person, the family, the institution and the community. However, visiting is not something that people always find easy to do. Those who have experienced an illness requiring rest in bed at home or in hospital will have met people like Jim who have visited partly out of duty, are clearly ill at ease, and can't wait for the visit to end. Although many visits are a great pleasure, with the visitor and the sick person benefiting enormously from the experience, it can still be a daunting task even when you know the sick person well.

There are so many disconcerting aspects to a visit. We may assume that the sick person will look and behave exactly as they usually do; we may not anticipate the changes produced by the illness or the embarassment of entering their bedroom and seeing them in nightdress or pyjamas. There may be all sorts of fears and anxieties about the nature of the illness, whether *we* might catch anything, fears about death and dying, or of some unpleasant confrontation arising from previous experience of the sick person. There may, as in Jim's case, be problems relating to communication and the feeling

60

that one 'ought to stay for a decent length of time' even if you run out of things to say after ten minutes. Fortunately in Betty MacDonald's case the other visitors did not experience this difficulty and the time passed quickly. On other occasions there may be a strong feeling of inadequacy which makes the visit a very painful experience.

Another influential factor is the capacity in which you visit: as a member of the family, friend, local clergyman, hospital chaplain, or voluntary lay visitor. This is especially relevant when considering the pastoral implications of visiting sick people, since the perceived role of the visitor is important to any understanding of the interaction between the sick person and visitor. To be allowed to share in someone else's experience at a time when they may feel vulnerable and anxious is one of the great privileges of pastoral care. The setting may make us feel uncomfortable and ill at ease, and the meeting itself may not be easy, but there are numerous occasions when it is enjoyable. If we can visit in a sensitive way, then it will frequently be a learning situation in which attitudes towards sickness, hospitals or individual people will be formed, challenged and re-shaped.

When undertaking general visiting it is important to introduce oneself clearly and explain why one is there. The conversation may remain at the level of generalities, such as the weather or hospital food, but the patient may indicate a desire to talk about forthcoming tests or operations. This general conversation may then lead to some form of agreement about how long one can stay and, later, whether or not the patient wishes you to visit again. On occasions there may be quite a formal agreement about such things as length and frequency of sessions, purpose of meeting and confidentiality which give the meeting a definite counselling structure (see article on 'Structure' [Blows, 1987]). It may also entail recognizing that pastor and client may meet in other settings and therefore the client may need reassuring that if the pastor says 'How are you?' no reference is being made to problems discussed within a counselling setting. This is important for chaplains who counsel staff within a hospital, in order to avoid embarrassment if they meet on a ward or in the lift. Respect for others will often be shown in the way in which we are careful over the management of boundary issues in pastoral care. Reference was made earlier (pp. 19—20) to the importance of boundaries in the pastor's own self-care. However, boundaries are also important *within* the pastoral relationship, since knowing that there is a structure provides a sense of security through defining a space which belongs to the patient/client who retains ownership of what happens within that space in terms of interaction, silence, rage, tears or walking out!

Many of the pastoral contacts we have with sick people are, however, of an informal nature and it can be difficult to maintain a clear distinction between pastoral and social contacts. This can lead to confusion over the purpose of pastoral visiting of patients in a general hospital ward when it is not at their invitation. Is the pastor there to convert and proselytize, to perform a religious ritual, to identify the dying, or to discuss the weather and hospital food? This confusion of purpose can link to a lack of clarity within the pastor as to who he/she is and why he/she is there and can eventually lead to the feeling that visiting is pointless. One way of resolving this is to be clear regarding the focus of pastoral care and pastoral visiting.

Focus in Pastoral Visiting

In an endeavour to clarify the purpose and focus of pastoral care Clebsch and Jaekle (1967) have defined it as 'helping acts, done by representative Christian persons, directed toward the healing, sustaining, guiding and reconciling of troubled persons whose troubles arise in the context of ultimate meanings and concerns' (op. cit., p. 4).

This definition, although written several years ago, has several helpful things to say about pastoral care in relation to times of sickness.

Firstly, Clebsch and Jaekle see pastoral care as a ministry performed by *representative Christian persons* who bring to bear upon human troubles the resources, wisdom and authority of the Christian faith and life. Thus pastoral care is concerned with the declaration of Christ's power to transform, heal and reconcile. This ministry may be performed by the ordained minister, lay members of the local congregation, or lay persons duly authorized and commissioned by the Church to exercise such a function and role. In some instances lay

people are involved in praying for healing and accompanying
the priest on some of his communion visits to the sick. This
would probably be in addition to any other visits they might
make to the same people, in an equally representative role.
The minister himself may exercise his pastoral care as pastor
to a particular congregation, or in connection with his/her
official role as a part-time or whole-time chaplain employed
by the local health authority. There is also another sense in
which the pastor is representative, in that his or her presence
may be endowed with powerful meaning and significance
because of the symbolic representations which a pastor may
bear. Blows (1987) indicates that the pastor can represent
many things to the person being visited, and consideration
should be given to the

> symbolic and transference significance of the pastor's role
> for the parishioner (as representative of God, the Church
> or parental figures) which may endow the pastor's presence
> (or absence) with powerful meaning. In the light of this
> there is a need to be aware of the implications for the
> parishioner of the behaviour of the pastor, e.g. regularity/
> irregularity, consistence/arbitrariness, giving/with-holding,
> and to structure behaviour accordingly. (Blows, p. 271)

This can sometimes be seen in the situation where a sick
person is experiencing a deep sense of unfairness and feels
angry with God for allowing such an illness to happen.
However, because the patient (as a child) could never express
anger which he felt towards his father he may therefore find
it virtually impossible to express this anger towards God (as
heavenly father). As a result the patient may become
depressed and withdrawn, or very compliant and eager to
please the pastor who 'represents' the powerful parent of
former years who you never shouted at in case something
worse should happen to you. If the pastor recognizes that he
is seen as representing this powerful parent he may be able to
explore the patient's feelings about the illness and gradually
enable some of the anger to be expressed:

PASTOR: *After general discussion which included some
statements by the patient that this illness is very untimely
and has spoilt holiday arrangements, family commitments*

etc. It sounds as though this illness has come at a bad time. I wonder what feelings you have at the moment?

PATIENT: Well. . . . (*pause*) . . . . . I mustn't grumble. When you look around here there are plenty worse off than me.

PASTOR: You sound very calm about the disruption, the money you think you might not get back for the holiday.

PATIENT: My wife's not so calm. She said it's not fair, but I told her not to talk like that . . . it doesn't do any good.

PASTOR: Your wife thinks it's unfair and is saying so, but you don't like people expressing such feelings.

PATIENT: Well I learnt years ago that those sort of feelings make matters worse. Also, I'm not sure I should be telling you all this.

PASTOR: You seem unsure what my reaction might be. Perhaps you could explain a bit more . . . (*etc.*).

In this brief dialogue the pastor is beginning to explore the patient's difficulty in sharing some of the reactions to the illness and to try and identify why this should be. The patient will either continue the exploration, if the relationship feels safe enough, or will change the subject and thank the pastor for the visit. Those wishing to explore the dynamic basis of the helping relationship, and the importance of insight into what both the pastor and the patient bring with them to the interaction, are recommended to read two very readable and practical books, Jacobs (1986) and Salzberger-Wittenberg (1986).

Secondly, the aim of pastoral care is to support and help *troubled persons* as individuals, and at times the focus for the pastor may be to support the troubled individual against the claims of the institution and group. We may even need to acknowledge that in some instances the needs of the individual cannot be reconciled with the needs of the institution. Similarly the cure of souls cannot be dictated by managerial or institutional requirements, since the cure of souls can only properly be exercised to the extent that the welfare of the individual can remain of prime importance. In the case of hospital chaplains (many of whom work whole-time within an institution) they may be caught up in trying to meet the expectations of various groups of people in conflict with each other. Frequently the only way through this dilemma is to clarify the *focus* of pastoral care rather than to ignore the institutional aspect. For example, in the midst of a major reorganization within the Health Service a chaplain may be caught between the needs of the individual seeking pastoral care and the needs of the institution which wishes to replace that individual with someone else. The institution may see the chaplain as someone who has an overview of the situation and therefore better able to appreciate the 'wisdom' of removing a particular individual from office and support the management in doing so. The individual may look to the chaplain as someone who can offer support and advice, but also perhaps be able to intercede with the organization on their behalf. Once again being clear about the aim and focus of pastoral care may be the only way of resolving (or living with) this tension and of teaching the institution about the distinctive nature of one's role.

Finally the definition offered by Clebsch and Jaekle states that the troubles with which the pastor may be called upon to help are usually those which arise out of *ultimate issues and concerns.* In the context of our ministry to sick people pastoral care, therefore, will relate to the search for meaning within the experience of sickness. If the pastoral relationship does not address itself to the search for meaning, and thus with spiritual concerns, then it cannot properly be described as *pastoral* care. It is interesting to note that Clebsch and Jaekle link 'helping acts' closely to healing, guiding, sustaining and reconciling, and involve questions of ultimate meaning. By this definition many 'helping acts' which people might otherwise perform may not be deemed as pastoral care in that they are not directed towards the same aim. It sometimes happens that engaging with the ultimate issues may be implicit rather than explicit. This is paralleled by the way in which at times one may engage with some aspect of spiritual distress (such as a sense of helplessness and hopelessness) without actually labelling it as a spiritual problem, whilst at other times one might clearly state that you are talking about and sharing an issue relating to the spiritual state of the person. This relates to the point made earlier regarding the confusion that can arise over the purpose of visiting.

Whilst it is possible to analyse the pastoral visiting of sick people from a social/psychological perspective there is also a very important theological/spiritual perspective to be considered. At the same time that attitudes may be challenged so may the assumptions and understanding of the visitor, which might be an uncomfortable experience. The visitor may find that he or she will experience some of the spiritual distress and search for meaning which the sick person is facing. This may lead to a desire to retreat, to decide not to visit again or not to get too involved.

Visiting is not, if I may use the expression, 'everyone's cup of tea' even if we all have to perform the task at some time. However, if we are undertaking visiting as a part of our pastorate and healing ministry, we need to know what we are about and to attempt to prepare ourselves accordingly. It is difficult to be sensitive and attentive when *we* are feeling anxious. Like Jim in *The Plague and I* our energy and our attention will be anywhere but on the *person* we are visiting. The only way in which we can be free or available for the other person is if we can be centred or rooted ourselves, both personally and in our relationship with God. The concept of the pastor/visitor creating a *space* which is safe and allows opportunity for feelings to be shared and expressed is especially relevant. The sick person is not necessarily a *passive recipient* of all that we in our seeming power and health have come to bestow. Frequently one finds that the sick person can and will give much to us if that space is available for both patient and visitor. One of the most humbling things about pastoral visits to the sick can be the way in which, on reflection, we find that the sick person has given us far more than we perhaps gave to them.

In the meeting between pastoral visitor and sick person God is already present and can reveal himself in and through the persons present who may, in faith, perceive him. The knowledge of the presence of God is something which we can relax into since it can free us to be ourselves in the meeting. This freedom to be ourselves with the other person (without having to play a part) can then enhance our ability to actively listen to what is being experienced by the patient and to be attentive to the amount of time we spend — not too long and not too short. Patients frequently try to look their best for visitors and may succumb to fatigue very quickly. The perceptive visitor will recognize this and either stay quietly making no demands or leave. But, as Causley (1983) has illustrated so graphically, visitors come in many different guises and not all will learn from the patient who often has a clear idea of what he or she expects. This is clear in the writing of Jo Anne Kelly Smith who was dying of cancer and wrote:

> When *anyone* comes to visit me, I don't want him to come with his own agenda . . . I often get the feeling that before people enter my room, they try to decide what to say. I don't want to hear their concerns. I want them to empty their heads of their own ideas. When you visit a sick person, fill your head with thoughts about that person, your care for him, and what you can do to get in touch with him . . . If you just go in and listen, they'll do all the 'saying' because they really want to talk about themselves. They need to get in touch with their feelings and they need to tell it to another human. (Smith, 1977, p. 112)

Over the years I have identified three broad areas of difficulty for people—*communication, feelings of inadequacy*, and *fear*—which we need to address in order to be more able to relate to the sick person in an open way.

Communication

Many visitors are not sure what to say, or not say, when visiting someone who is sick, especially if the prognosis is poor or uncertain. It can lead to awkwardness between people which may be dealt with in various ways. Sometimes those close to the sick person will act as a shield to protect the patient from those who would unthinkingly, or deliberately, try to acquaint the person with the true state of affairs. This often sets up undercurrents which the patient may well spot even if they are not commented upon. This has important pastoral implications when the pastor may feel very constrained by other people from clear and open communication with the sick person. (See Ainsworth-Smith and Speck, 1982, p. 28f.)

A person's culture can be an additional factor in making a visit an uncomfortable experience. An Indian lady told me of her feelings whilst a hospital patient:

> When I was a patient in a mission hospital in India I had
> more friends and relatives come to visit me then than I had
> ever seen before. I was in for a very minor operation, but
> my father and mother-in-law came about 100 miles to stay
> with my husband for a few days. My mother-in-law spent
> the whole day sitting by my side. All the people who came
> to see me were friends or relatives of *hers*, and I think they
> came more to show their respect for her than to see me.
> Friends of my father-in-law came too, but they were too
> embarrassed to speak to me lying in bed—instead, they
> congregated outside the ward smoking and reminiscing.

Since many of the friends could not cope with the
embarrassment they escaped, and thus communicated to the
patient more than they were perhaps intending to. Such
embarrassment may also be overcome by humour, as
illustrated by many of the get-well cards and messages one
sees on a bedside cabinet or locker. The rather basic/earthy
type of humour encountered in certain hospital wards is
another way of coping with the anxiety or embarrassment
associated with some illnesses or investigations. Whilst
humour can have a healing, transforming effect it can also be
very hurtful or, on occasions, may become a 'gallows' humour:
for example, the elderly man who knew he was dying and
whose wife had, according to local gossip, always worked
him hard said to me, 'Have you heard the latest? When I die
she [his wife] is planning to have me cremated and put in an
hour-glass. So I'll even have to work after I've gone!'

Sometimes communication is a problem because the sick
person has had a stroke or some illness which affects the
ability to speak or respond. Many visitors find it very difficult
to hold a conversation when there is little by way of response.
Similarly, unless in the privacy of their own home,
communicating in a loud voice with the deaf can be
embarrassing. Bellowing 'words of comfort' to someone who
is frightened quickly leads to an awareness of how empty
certain phrases sound in such situations. This may lead us to
retreat rapidly, to communicate by touch or some other way,
or to silently 'be with' the person who is afraid. There are, of
course, those visitors who always hold a one-way conversation
and give the other person little opportunity to respond, or

they reply on behalf of the sick person. 'How are you today?'
. . . 'The Vicar's asking how you are. You're much better
aren't you. Say your prayers every night, don't you dear?'

Visiting someone who is unwilling or unable to respond
does make one self-conscious, but it can be important to try
to communicate even if it is only one way. For example: a
young girl was admitted to a psychiatric hospital and was
diagnosed as having an hysterical disorder. She withdrew
completely into herself and would not talk, smile or dress,
and later became incontinent. I took the mother to visit her
daughter and on the way to the hospital the mother explained
how inadequate she felt at getting no response from her
daughter. It was a very hot day and her daughter was in a hot
woollen dress. Without resistance the girl, for the first time,
allowed her mother to change her dress for a cotton one. She
did not speak to her mother during the afternoon. After
visiting some other people I subsequently collected the mother
and spoke *to* the girl. On the way home the mother kept
saying, 'I feel so much better. She let me change her. She let
me change her.' Then she said, 'She knew you, you know. I
could see it in her eyes.' Three months later the daughter was
discharged from hospital and came to see me. She told me
that she remembered my visit and had known who I was. She
had wanted to thank me, and for taking her mother, but the
words would not come out. Similar things have been said by
patients thought to be totally unconscious but who later
recover; therefore we must beware of assuming that
communication is pointless.

Communication problems often arise because of the
assumptions we make about another person's experience.
Thus we may easily say the 'wrong' thing because it is based
on what we have assumed and not on what the sick person
has shared with us. For example, the young woman who has
suffered with an ulcerated bowel for many years may have
lost a lot of opportunities at school or work because of ill
health. If she eventually comes into hospital for an operation
resulting in an ileostomy, so that body waste is now
discharged into a bag attached to her stomach wall, we might
assume that she will be deeply upset and unable to cope. This
may well be an initial reaction, but as she regains her health
and finds that she is fitter than she has ever been she may

later be very pleased with the results of the operation. What we might say at one stage of recovery may not be appropriate at another stage. We may sometimes seem insensitive because the timing is wrong and we have not allowed the sick person to share what *they* feel before we respond. Listening needs to precede responding if pastoral communication is to be effective. (See Jacobs, 1985.)

On those occasions when we do say the 'wrong' thing it is often better to acknowledge that, to apologize, and accept whatever reaction is produced rather than to leave and never return. When we feel anxious, tired or angry in a situation it is very easy for us, the sick person or the family, to express things in a way not originally intended. The pain caused by this can be acute, but the hurt can be healed if one or more of the persons concerned can acknowledge what has happened and try to work through it.

Communication is not, of course, only concerned with words. Whether we are using words or not, much is being conveyed by non-verbal means. Our approach to the person tells them a great deal even before we speak. One dying person told me he had learnt the language of eyes. 'They approach my bed with smiling mouths, but their eyes are sad. I know I'm dying.' To stand at the end of the bed and expect an intimate and personal discussion is unrealistic and conveys the message that we don't really want to know. Sitting close to the person and in a position that does not necessitate their twisting their neck to look up is also important. Direct continual eye contact can be intimidating but there does need to be a reasonable degree of eye contact to establish rapport and show that we are attentive to the person we are with. If communication is difficult, and we are not attentive to the person we have come to visit, it is not long before the other patients and activities in the ward become far more interesting than the person we originally came to visit! The visitor may feel guilty about producing some knitting, or a newspaper and just sitting quietly with the patient. In some situations it can help if the pastor or the sick person can 'give permission' to the visitor to knit, read or watch television without feeling guilty that they should be constantly *doing* something while they visit.

It is also easier to visit if you have something to take for the person visited. This is true under normal social conditions but is especially true when sick-visiting. People usually find it difficult simply to take themselves and so arrive with grapes, flowers, books, magazines and chocolates. Such gifts may simply be an expression of caring, and of a need to *do* something, even though the patient does not like grapes and has hay fever. Such gifts may also be a way of expressing the inexpressible, since some people may find it very difficult to say in words what they really want to say and so will do so with gifts and flowers instead. At times they may be placatory to ward off antagonism or expiate guilt for past omissions or arguments, and such gifts are often seen by the recipient for what they are!

Touch is also a very vital form of communication. In a poem by Anthony Thwaite there is an account of the visit of a father to a sick child. The visit is made at night, the light is dim and the shadows long and dark.

Sick Child

Lit by the small night-light you lie
And look through swollen eyes at me:
Vulnerable, sleepless, try
To stare through a blank misery,
And now that boisterous creature I
Have known so often shrinks to this
Wan ghost unsweetened by a kiss.

Shaken with retching, bewildered by
The virus curdling milk and food,
You do not scream in fear, or cry.
Tears are another thing, a mood
Given an image, infancy
Making permitted show of force,
Boredom, or sudden pain. The source

Of this still vacancy's elsewhere.
Like my sick dog, ten years ago,
Who skulked away to some far lair
With poison in her blood: you know
Her gentleness, her clouded stare,
Pluck blankets as she scratched the ground.
She made, as you now make, no sound.

The rank smell shrouds you like a sheet.
Tomorrow we must let crisp air
Blow through the room and make it sweet,
Making all new. I touch your hair,
Damp where your forehead sweats, and meet—
Here by the door as I leave you—
A cold, quiet wind, chilling me through.

(Thwaite, 1963)

Although there is no spoken communication with the child a great deal has been communicated to the father and his own deep feelings have been expressed in the simple gesture, 'I touch your hair'. Touching hair, holding hands, smoothing the brow, helping to wash or feed someone who is sick, holding a vomit bowl can all convey a degree of concern depending upon how they are performed. Making physical contact can be very important pastorally, especially when the sick person may feel very isolated and lonely by reason of the illness. The sacramental aspect of touch should not be underestimated in contexts other than the formal 'laying on of hands', in that restoration, acceptance, and genuine care can often be best conveyed through touch rather than words.

Feelings of Inadequacy

When someone is ill the relatives may feel helpless to care for them in the way they would wish to. In the case of a minor illness this does not become too great a problem in that the sick person is often able to do a great deal for themselves. Even so, there are instances where you desperately wish you could bring relief. A parent sitting up for most of the night in a hot steamy bathroom trying to bring relief to a child with an attack of asthma or croup can feel very inadequate in spite of medical advice and drugs which, at that moment, don't seem to be working. The relative of someone suffering from a depressive illness may find it hard to understand what the person is experiencing or how best to respond and therefore feel equally disabled as a result.

When the sick person is admitted to hospital the relatives may feel relieved that the hospital has 'taken over', but others may feel guilty that the relative is now beyond their care and that there is apparently nothing they can do. This is sometimes compounded by the patient berating the relatives for 'putting me in such a place'. Because of this feeling of inadequacy the relatives often assume a critical approach to the care given by the hospital. A relative may 'inspect' the patient and then comment or complain that he/she would not be left looking unshaven, and without teeth or glasses, were they still at home — in spite of the patient being on intensive care and with tubes in mouth and nose. Whilst such criticism may be very trying for the staff, the relative/visitor is really saying: 'If only I could do something. I feel so helpless and being critical of standards of care is the only way I can show I still care.' From the viewpoint of pastoral care the pastor may feel an inner pressure, because of inadequacy in the face of suffering, to promise too much to the sick person as an unconscious effort to compensate for being fit and well.

Many visitors find it easier to visit if they can do something while they are there. To sit on a chair at the side of the bed for two hours looking at the patient, the drip stand, the catheter bag or the temperature chart is alien to most people. If the visit is to the home then it may be possible for the visitor to do various tasks for the sick person — such as making a cup of tea, arranging flowers, vaccuuming or dusting a room, arranging to do some shopping, giving the person a wash or a bath, or washing their hair. Such activities are not so easily performed in hospital, unless the unit encourages some relatives to share in the care of the patients. Certainly in some instances the relatives are more expert than the staff in knowing how to care for people with certain conditions because they have had years of experience of coping at home. Much anger can be generated if hospital staff imply that the patient's readmission is the result of inadequate care at home.

If the person who is sick is in great pain, conversation may not be possible or appropriate and the visitor may feel more helpless. Pain has a great tendency to isolate people from others and the ability of a visitor simply to be there quietly may ease some of the fear engendered by the pain (see Autton, 1986). Fussiness and over-activity can add to the pain, as anyone with a headache can testify. As one patient commented, when he found himself surrounded by 'busy people' — 'I wish people would *just come*, and not fuss about.' If the person is ill at home the next of kin may have spent long hours sitting by the bedside *being with* the sick person. The relative may be reluctant to leave even for a short while lest there is a change in the patient's condition. The feeling of inadequacy coupled with anxiety may make it very difficult for a relative to consider their own need of sleep and food. Part of the pastoral care in such a situation might be the arranging of night sitters from the local church who could take over from the relative for a short while. The need to feel that you have done everything possible for the person who is ill is a very powerful force even when the relationship has been ambivalent. Not all relationships are loving and kind, and there can sometimes be a great sense of obligation to care even when one doesn't especially 'like' the person in need. This can create resentment and guilt in the person who is caring, which may be worked out in different ways: for example, the guilt which can be generated by an ambivalent relationship may cause relatives either to take on far more than they can manage or to over-indulge the patient as a means of expiating their guilt.

Fear

Many years ago Michel Quoist graphically described the bewilderment and uncertainty of visiting a sick parishioner in a hospital ward:

The hospital

> This afternoon I went to see a patient at the hospital.
> From ward to ward I walked, through that city of
>   suffering, sensing the tragedies hardly concealed by the
>   brightly painted walls and the flower-bordered lawns.
> I had to go through a ward; I walked on tiptoe, hunting for
>   my patient.
> My eyes passed quickly and discreetly over the sick, as one
>   touches a wound delicately to avoid hurting.
> I felt uncomfortable,
> Like the uninitiated traveller lost in a mysterious temple,
> Like a pagan in the nave of a church.

At the very end of the second ward I found my patient,
And once there, I could only stammer. I had nothing to say.
(Quoist, 1965)

These feelings have been echoed by many other visitors who
have walked down a ward in search of the patient, or walked
up to the door of the house wondering what awaited them on
the inside.

> On the first visit I entered the main hospital with
> trepidation and a certain amount of foreboding brought on,
> possibly, by fear of the unknown and also by the fact that
> this was a very old establishment. It was originally an
> asylum . . . My fears were not dispelled as I walked along
> the dingy-looking tiled corridors to the admission ward
> where my wife was. I had noticed one or two men standing
> about the corridors — dejected, pathetic looking people who
> gazed upon me as I passed, or if they didn't ask for fags
> appeared to look through me, with not a flicker of emotion
> on their faces. I asked myself, 'God, what is this place I
> have come to and why is my wife here?' I felt more than a
> little uneasy and somewhat frightened.

Once this visitor had entered the ward and experienced the
support and help of a cheerful staff he was able to overcome
his initial fear (Speck, 1970). The physical surroundings can
be daunting to many people and make it very difficult for
them to visit sick people within an institution. They may also
be afraid of what they might see. Illness can alter a person's
appearance and this can be distressing for some people, as
seen with some forms of cancer. Sometimes the alteration is
to the personality, as in some forms of mental illness, where
the person seems to respond and react in a totally different
way. Patients who have undergone disfiguring surgery often
describe the reactions of their visitors when they see them for
the first time. One elderly man who had had radical surgery
to the face and neck because of a cancer of the jaw described
the first visit of his son. The son had been briefed by the
ward staff as to the temporary nature of the change in his
father's appearance and what he would look like. However,
on entering the room the son was very shocked by what he
saw. His father said, 'I could see in his face I looked bloody

awful. Then he said he had to go out for a minute . . . and I heard him being sick in the corridor. I just wished I could die.' The staff of the ward worked very hard to help father and son share their feelings about what had happened, and they were able to overcome the shock and the hurt surrounding this incident.

There may be a very real fear of disease and corruption leading to avoidance of sick people as far as possible. This fear might be heightened by the unexpected sight of apparatus such as drips (blood or glucose), nasogastric and drainage tubes, monitors and ventilator machines. By avoiding such visits we may be able to pretend that physical, mental illness or old age don't really exist. An elderly lady was admitted to a geriatric unit for a few weeks following a fall. On her return home her teenage grand-daughter said, 'Do you know why I didn't come to visit you? I couldn't face seeing myself when I was old.'

If the person has an infectious or contagious disease necessitating barrier nursing, this may create anxiety of what the visitor might catch from the patient. Whilst sensible precautions should be taken, the isolating effect of some forms of illness can only be overcome by a willingness to overcome the fear and relate to the person. When Jesus touched the man who had leprosy (Luke 5.13) he not only restored him physically but he also restored him socially and as a person. It is important pastorally that we do not lose sight of the *person* who has AIDS or hepatitis or typhoid and, because of our own fear, add to their feeling of alienation.

The fear of death and dying may also inhibit some people from visiting. If we find the prospect of personal death too disturbing we will usually keep well clear of the dying, for their presence will confront us with what we wish to deny or avoid. As mentioned elsewhere (Ainsworth-Smith and Speck 1982), visiting the dying will awaken any ambivalent feelings between patient and visitor; conflict and a sense of guilt may develop and perhaps subconscious anger—not least with the dying for dying and therefore making us feel this way!

If we have an antagonistic relationship with the person we are visiting, then we are not likely to look forward to the visit. In an early novel by Paul Bailey (1967) we meet Mrs Gadny, a widow, whose daughter Celia has recently died of leukaemia. Mrs Gadny goes to live with her sullen stepson,

Henry, and his selfish wife, Thelma. She is cared for out of a sense of duty and eventually is transferred into an old people's home, 'The Jerusalem'—a green-and-white-tiled former workhouse. She is repulsed by the place and feels trapped there. Against this background we have an account of a visit by Thelma and Henry on a hot summer day when, outwardly, all appears happy and well, but we are given glimpses of some of the feelings going on underneath for all three people.

'Perhaps she's refused to see us, Henry.' Thelma was hopeful. [As the visit continues Mrs Gadny's resentment mounts.] She spoke slowly. 'Whatever you say, Thelma, I've been disposed of.' An image came. 'Like trash, waste.' [And later she bangs her fists on the box of chocolates on her lap—] 'Have your bloody chocolates, Thelma. Have the bloody things.' She did not give them back. 'Is the inspection over? I can still stand, I still walk, I've eaten, I've slept, I've had bloody baths . . .'
Thelma's fears of accusation were well founded.

Visiting sick people would seem to have the effect of exposing the vulnerabilities of the various people concerned. This can sometimes be a painful experience, especially if the previous relationship has been difficult. The anxieties we may have about sickness, hospitals, and dying may all contribute to a sense of discomfort.

> The fifth, a giant from the fields
> With suit smelling of milk and hay,
> Shifts uneasily from one bullock foot
> To the other, as though to avoid
> Settling permanently in the antiseptic landscape.
>
> Occasionally he looses a scared glance
> Sideways, as though fearful of what intimacy
> He may blunder on, or that the walls
> Might suddenly close in on him.
>
> He carries flowers, held lightly in fingers
> The size and shape of plantains,
> Tenderly kisses his wife's cheek
> — The brush of a child's lips—
> Then balances, motionless, for thirty minutes
> On the thin chair.

At the end of visiting time
He emerges breathless,
Blinking with relief, into the safe light.

He does not appear to notice
The dusk.

(Causley, 1983)

In caring for those who are sick we must ensure that those who visit and look after them are not neglected but receive appropriate support for themselves. This might be in terms of transport to and from the local hospital, meals, assistance with washing clothes, interpretation of the illness and patient's behaviour, and providing the necessary space for the visitor to share what they are feeling and experiencing. This can be as important a part of pastoral care as focusing on the sick person alone, since it can enhance the health of the family and caring group and perhaps prevent them becoming patients alongside the patient. (See chapter 10, 'Supporting Those Who Care'.)

The pastoral visiting that has been discussed in this chapter might be undertaken by a variety of people and not necessarily clergy. There is a sense in which the *pastoral* visitor is a representative of the local community, the Church and of Christ (see pp. 62−3). The clergy and people of the local congregation may form a pastoral team expressing a concern for the health and healing of the entire community in partnership with others involved with health care. The representative aspect of the visitor and the importance of the variety of local church/lay visiting schemes will be the focus of the next chapter.

SIX

The Church Is Visiting — Lay Visiting Schemes

═══════

The function of the professionals is not to act as examples to be imitated or to instruct the volunteers in the art of psychotherapy, but to encourage them to develop the skills which they already possess and to help them to a deeper understanding of the people whom they are visiting. (Dyne, 1981, p.8)

Visiting the sick may be seen as one individual visiting another individual either because of genuine loving concern, or out of family duty, neighbourliness or because of professional involvement. However, these people are also representatives of the groups they have come from. There is a sense in which the patient, the doctor, the nurse, social worker, ward orderly, health visitor, local church visitor, relative are all representative of the society, community, family, church or professional group to which they belong. The pastor may represent other things at an irrational level, such as the judge, or the undertaker. In the meeting between the sick person, the visitor, and those who are there to heal and support, the resourcefulness of the individual is being tested, as is the resourcefulness of the groups in society which they each represent. As the late R. A. Lambourne expressed it:

> . . . in every encounter of man with man, in every giving and receiving, Christ's presence is fourfold. He is the sick man, the prisoner, the child, the stranger. He is the giver of the cup of water, the clothes, the *visitor*. He is the one who preaches the Gospel. He is the one who receives those who preach the Gospel. (Lambourne, 1963, p. 48 — my italics)

This is not intended to make sick-visiting into a pious activity but to indicate another aspect to visiting which, on occasions, may be clearly evident alongside the genuine loving concern being shown by one person visiting another at a time of sickness. It is relevant to note that there is a semantic link between the word 'visit' as used in Matthew 25.36, 'I was sick, and you visited me' ($\epsilon\pi\epsilon\sigma\kappa\epsilon\psi\alpha\sigma\theta\epsilon$), and that used to describe God's visitation of his people as in Luke 1.68 'Blessed be the Lord God of Israel; for he has visited and redeemed his people' ($\epsilon\pi\epsilon\sigma\kappa\epsilon\psi\alpha\tau o$). Thus the person who visits the sick may also reflect what God is doing in visiting his people. The pastoral visitor represents God and his Church, in that he or she visits as a member of the Body of Christ and so expresses both that humanity cares and that Christ cares. It may be appropriate to share our knowledge of God's presence with the person we are visiting, but sensitivity is the keyword in seeking to achieve this. It may well be that it is the sick person who makes this known to us. Ramsay (1969) described such encounters as 'disclosure events'. At times the visitor may act as the 'enabler' who helps those in the situation to apprehend the presence of the living Christ and, in accepting him, to be joined to him within a fellowship of love which has the power to heal and save. The pastoral care of the sick must, therefore, be seen as far wider than the ministry of an individual clergyman within a hospital or the community. Rather it is a corporate activity of the whole Church, as the Body of Christ, loving, reconciling and healing, and thus providing the sort of environment in which sick people can regain their physical, mental and spiritual health.

This corporate aspect of pastoral care has led to the development of pastoral teams within a particular locality, which might be centred upon one particular church or be developed ecumenically by members of various churches within the area. Such teams concern themselves with a variety of pastoral activities, including support for the bereaved, visiting of those seeking the occasional offices of the church, the setting-up and staffing of a counselling service, inter-cessory prayer groups, and the visiting and support of sick people and their families.

The role of sick-visiting may be fairly informal, in that members of a congregation may 'keep an eye on' the residents in their particular road or block of flats and, in times of sickness, either offer help in a 'sensitive' (and not nosey!) neighbourly way or, with the permission of the family, inform the local pastor/priest who may then visit. In many parts of the country such informal schemes have provided valuable support to the elderly, the chronic sick, the anxious and the lonely.

Such befriending has done much to prevent illness developing in many instances and has been a very important part of health care within a particular district. To be discharged from hospital is not always welcome news to the housebound, the aged or the lonely. Knowing that you have a neighbour who can get the house/flat warm for you and see that there is milk, bread and other food available can make all the difference. Similarly, knowing that there is someone whom you can telephone or who will call round for a chat can help overcome the isolation which frequently follows dis-charge from hospital where there is always someone to talk to or to offer help if required.

The Church, of course, does not have the sole prerogative for such caring, but wherever possible the Church *should* be seen to be caring. In addition to the above tasks the 'street warden' may also, through the local church, be able to arrange for visits from the church or for those who are chronically sick or disabled to be taken out for a drive, or to church if practically possible. The changing patterns of life in our society have affected the various 'street warden' schemes established years ago. Whilst some of these schemes still operate in many areas it has proved very difficult to establish such ventures in some of our inner city areas.

The health problems in urban priority areas have been referred to in the report of the Archbishop of Canterbury's Commission, entitled *Faith in the City* (1985) which reached the conclusion that:

> The people who live in urban priority areas are less healthy and less well provided for than people who live in other more prosperous areas . . . Overall, the relationship between social deprivation and health is seen in higher rates of death, illness, admission to psychiatric hospitals, suicides, and accidents in the UPAs than in the rest of the country. (Sections 11.1, 11.8)

In its recommendations regarding the provision of health care the report stressed that the Church must promote a broader understanding of the meaning of health in terms of wholeness. It should give help and encouragement to neighbourhood projects since these would benefit the health of vulnerable groups and be an immediate practical outworking of such theological concerns as the biblical concepts of 'Shalom' and wholeness. The Church is present in every neighbourhood and so, in order to be better acquainted with the needs of the area it serves, the local church should undertake an 'audit' as part of its response to the report. Such an audit will also need to reflect future plans within the area surveyed in the light of policy decisions at government and local level relating to community care, especially in respect of psychiatric illness. Just as the report calls upon the government to ensure that adequate resources are available to provide proper locally-based support services for vulnerable and handicapped people and their carers, so the Church is also expected to respond by involving itself in such provision. Such community work is seen 'as a legitimate lay ministry. It is an important expression of concern for one's neighbour-in-community, which is as essential to discipleship as the worship to which it is integrally related.' (Section 12.49)

Therefore, whatever difficulties may face the Church, it is being called upon to continue to involve itself with the neighbourhood in which it is situated and to co-operate with all agencies (voluntary and statutory) who seek to enhance the health of that community. It is partly against this background, and partly in its 'representative role', that we should set the Church's establishment of groups of people who can share in the visiting and pastoral care of the sick.

Visiting Teams

In a variety of places specific teams have been established for visiting sick and disabled people whether they are at home, in hospital, or in a community-care home or long-stay unit within the area. These teams may be based at a local church or may be attached to the chaplaincy of a local hospital. In some instances, where the chaplain is also the minister of the local church, the team will have a clear link with both hospital and church. This is very much in keeping with section 12.20 of *Faith in the City* which advocates that the church should support and train its members to provide a service in this way: 'This may be in relation to meeting the needs of bereaved people, of handicapped people, or responding to problems of housing, local transport, schooling or policing and neighbour-hood.'

Visiting the sick can be very demanding in a physical, emotional and spiritual sense. It is important, therefore, that any group undertaking this form of ministry should be fully aware of what they are taking on and feel that they have the necessary support to continue with it. Various schemes have been devised in different parts of the country, providing training courses of varying intensity. A prerequisite of any such scheme is to be clear about why one is needed and who needs to be consulted before one is set up. In hospital and home visiting the provision of unhurried visits is high in priority together with a recognition of the limits of pastoral involvement before referral to the minister, chaplain or parish priest is indicated. Within the hospital setting the proposals should be discussed at an early stage with chaplaincy colleagues, the appropriate management groups, health authority, and church authorities. Where a hospital has a Voluntary Services Organizer there should be close liaison since volunteers need to be registered for insurance purposes before undertaking any tasks on hospital premises. It is desirable that such a pastoral visiting scheme should be on an ecumenical basis if at all possible, since this helps to harmonize such work with the representational aspect of pastoral care. The backing of local churches is also important, since it is mainly from them that people will be recruited.

Visiting people you know can be daunting at times and to visit sick people you may never have met before can make the visitor feel even more anxious. Therefore there needs to be an appropriate form of selection, training and support for such people. In respect of pastoral visiting in hospitals the Training Support Group of the Hospital Chaplaincies Council (HCC) has produced a valuable guide to the introduction of 'chaplaincy visitors' (HCC, 1986). These very clear guidelines reflect the considerable experience of several hospital chaplains who have implemented such schemes. The word 'selection' is anathema to some people since it obviously implies that some people may not be selected for the task and may subsequently feel hurt or rejected. However, it has to be clearly recognized that not everyone who offers to become a 'chaplaincy visitor' is necessarily best suited to that particular pastoral task and may, perhaps, be better directed elsewhere. Within church life clergy sometimes find it difficult to turn people down and may experience feelings of guilt if they do not accept everyone who offers their services. However, there are times when this is necessary. For example, if the individual has recently been bereaved and therefore the timing is wrong, or in the course of the training programme it may emerge that the person has gifts and talents that may be better used elsewhere. Great care should be exercised over those who are not selected to minimize feelings of failure and hurt.

In common with many such undertakings the HCC guide makes it clear that the initial selection is *only for training* and does not imply any obligation or commitment to the final task by either party. The selection is best done by interview with a small group of people from various disciplines within the hospital. Whilst the interview may be informal the panel does need to satisfy itself as to the motivation of the candidate and his/her awareness of strengths and weaknesses, sensitivity to other people's needs and general suitability. The latter is difficult to define but has much to do with the initial impression made, the outward appearance and the ability to listen and to communicate clearly. The credibility of the visitor, the chaplain, and not least of the Church, can depend on how such visitors are able to relate to those caring professionally for the sick as well as relating to the sick people they will be visiting. Therefore, having been selected, the volunteers will then commence their training.

Training and Support

The use of the word 'training' may make this sound very formal and imply an over-professionalizing of what they have to offer, but if people are to share in a very important aspect of pastoral care it is vital that they feel reasonably prepared for what they might experience. The words of Dyne at the beginning of this chapter are relevant here since we must beware of 'training out' the very essential qualities or skills that the non-professional can bring to such a situation.

> The function of the professionals in not to act as examples to be imitated or to instruct the volunteers in the art of psychotherapy, but to encourage them to develop the skills which they already possess and to help them to a deeper understanding of the people whom they are visiting. (Dyne, 1981)

By drawing on the experience of various clergy who have established such visiting schemes, the HCC guide outlines the content of such a training programme with due attention being paid to structures and to the mutual expectations of the people concerned (see Appendix B for suggested topics). Since many of these expectations may be unrealistic, and expectations are a common cause of stress in pastoral work, time must be given to examining and reflecting carefully on this area together with the very important topic of confidentiality. The resourcefulness of the visitor will also be tested by the patient and the staff and this may be on a spiritual and a personal level. Once again, Causley's reflections can provide useful material for discussion of various types of encounter! Whatever training or practical experience is undertaken, there needs to be some form of final selection which is linked to a formal recognition and commissioning.

A suitable liturgical rite of passage is necessary before the visitors begin their work. They need a formal recognition by hospital and Church that they are now authorized for their pastoral role under the guidance of the chaplain, who has also been duly appointed by the Church and hospital authority to exercise a ministry there. In the course of the commissioning service the representational aspect of the 'chaplaincy visitor' can be underlined, and all such services will offer a useful opportunity for the teaching of both Church and hospital concerning the spiritual care of sick people and those who look after them. Once the visitors begin their work they will need regular meetings with the chaplain for feedback, for support and further training as required. Meeting together as a group for worship, a meal, or discussion can be of great benefit to the chaplain as well as the visitor. It may also, however, be challenging if not threatening to the chaplains if such groups raise issues which the chaplains find painful. A very useful way of looking at the interaction between sick person and pastoral visitor is provided by a list produced by the Revd Ian Ainsworth-Smith, Chaplain to St George's Hospital, London; it is reproduced here with his permission.

'Maybe there are better ways than to . . .'
1. Assume that, because the patient is going home, he is happy about it.
2. Believe the patient literally when she says, 'I'm just fine'.
3. Assume the patient loves his family, and family loves him.
4. Introduce the subject of Church affiliation.
5. Flatter the patient, either pure unadulterated, or subtle.
6. Avoid conversation about the patient's illness when the patient introduces it.
7. Be interested in the patient's physical condition more than emotional experience.
8. Tell the patient he looks well or good. (Looks can be deceiving.)
9. Talk about our own family problems.
10. Preach little 'sermonettes'.
11. Apologise for making a call on the patient; being lax; being too busy.
12. Ask the patient, 'What's wrong with you?'
13. Talk about ourselves—our interests.
14. Gather a large amount of statistical information about the patient.
15. Tell the patient what her feelings ought to be.
16. Mumble indistinctly own name on introduction.
17. When the patient says, 'I'm afraid,' reply, 'You shouldn't be afraid'.
18. Ask medical questions without using the answer therapeutically.
19. Ask 'loaded' questions—'You don't think *that* do you?'
20. Change the subject whenever the patient cries or talks of subjects filled with emotion.

21. Defend God, Christ, Church when these subjects are under attack.
22. Win an argument, but lose the patient.
23. Defend the hospital, doctors, nurses, procedures.
24. Reprimand or scold the patient, either directly or by implication.
25. Give premature reassurance, or reassurance where we have no authority.
26. Offer a 'What can I do for you?' or 'service' approach to the patient.
27. Assume, because the patient is in hospital, that he is going to have an operation.
28. Tell the patient you had same illness/surgery and there's 'nothing to it'.
29. Say 'Would you care for me to say a prayer?'—make the patient responsible.
30. Break a pause by changing the subject or talking.
31. Reveal to the patient that we have information about him/her.
32. Sit down before being invited by the patient.
33. Fail to respond to the patient's feelings when they have opened their heart to us.
34. Agree with the patient when actually we don't agree.
35. Direct the conversation along our line.
36. Try to carry out a visit with two patients at the same time.
37. Try to direct the conversation around to God or a subject which interests us.
38. Become impatient with a long-winded, tedious, boring patient.
39. Be so self-conscious of our role that we lose sight of the patient.
40. Reveal too much of our own feelings, e.g. 'That's too bad!'
41. Insert personal comments, interests, mutual acquaintances.
42. Become so distressed by the patient's condition that we hurry away.
43. Think of ourselves as a 'problem solver'.
44. Jump too quickly to discussion of the future in a bereavement situation.

45. Give the impression we are in a hurry or on a 'time schedule'.
46. Try to 'cheer up' the patient.
47. Become pleased and blinded by flattery patient offers us.
48. Visit when relatives of the patient are present.
49. Jump ahead of the patient's emotional mood or level.
50. Respond to what the patient 'says' rather than to 'feelings' underlying what is said.

This list of things that we might say or do when visiting the sick is relevant for chaplains as well as lay visitors, since all of us will recognize situations where we have acted in a similar fashion. The purpose of this list is not to create such guilt or feelings of uselessness that we are de-skilled or disabled by the exercise. Rather it is intended to heighten our sensitivity and enable us to be more reflective about our responses to the various things that might happen when visiting. This list is, therefore, a catalyst to discussion rather than a list of things to avoid in *all* circumstances. For example:

Item 12: Ask the patient, 'What's wrong with you?'
Nosiness about other people's ailments can be a good substitute for genuine concern about what the person may be feeling and experiencing, especially if we do not use the information in any therapeutic way. There are some circumstances when it may be very relevant to find out, from the patient, what they think is wrong with them. If the patient has a malignant disease it can help the chaplain to relate more realistically if he/she knows what the patient knows and understands about the illness. This can be elicited by a question such as 'What have the doctors been able to tell you so far?' which is an 'open-ended' question allowing a brief 'They never tell you anything' or a detailed description of the diagnosis and prognosis, depending on what the patient knows *or wishes to share.*

Item 17: When the patient says, 'I'm afraid,' reply, 'You shouldn't be afraid'.
It is very easy to offer reassurance to someone in such a way

that we make them feel guilty for not being as strong, courageous or filled with faith as we appear to be. Part of creating a 'safe space' for the other person entails allowing them to share whatever they are feeling without that feeling being judged. It may be that we then go on to find out what they are afraid of and to look at how real those fears are. For example, a young expectant mother, in hospital with high blood pressure, spent much of the day crying and seemed reluctant to explain why. When the chaplain arrived on the ward, in desperation the ward sister said, 'Please, will you have a go—everyone else has!' After a while the lady said, 'I'm afraid for my children . . . because of my husband.' When invited to explain what was happening she gradually said, between sobs, 'When he feeds the budgie, he pours the seed over the top of the cage . . .' Unsure how to respond to this the chaplain said, 'Yes . . .' She then said, 'Well, if that's how my husband is looking after the budgie while I'm in here, what's he doing to the house and the kids?'—and she dissolved in tears again. Clearly, at visiting time, there was a need for someone to talk to husband and wife so that she could receive the reassurance she needed. By listening to her story the staff were able to understand the grounds of her fear.

By letting the patients explain, rather than telling them not to be afraid, we can then establish if there are grounds for their anxiety. Thus, in another situation, the sick person may have seen other patients on the ward return from the same test/investigation or operation that they await and so they know better than we do what lies ahead. On the other hand, their condition may be quite different and not comparable to that of the patient in the next bed. Some patients who develop a cancer may be very afraid of dying because twenty years ago a relative had a very unpleasant death from cancer which convinces the patient that they will have the same experience. Reassurance about modern symptom relief, etc. may ease the anxiety, but only after we have listened and understood the grounds for the fear.

Item 36: Try to carry out a visit with two patients at the same time.

In some wards this is difficult to avoid, in that patients may be sitting together as a group when you enter the ward. If you do not know any of the people in the group it may be necessary to talk generally with the group by introducing yourself and explaining why you are there. To focus on one person and exclude them from the group may embarrass them and seem intrusive to the others. In such situations it may be better to be alert to anyone leaving the group and returning quietly to their own bed in case they are, non-verbally, indicating a wish to talk with you on their own — or to escape from your visit! However, to stand between two beds and try to converse with both people in order to cut down on the time you need to spend in that ward is a different matter.

Item 40: Reveal too much of our own feelings, e.g. 'That's too bad!'

When listening to a sick person it can be very tempting to openly react to what they are saying. There is a fine line between responding 'empathically' and overloading the sick person with our own response. 'You did *what*? or, 'You poor thing, if I were you I'd have kicked him out years ago!' The key in this item is the phrase 'too much' since, in order to develop the relationship, it is important to show the other person that their feelings are valued by reflecting back to them what we have picked up. 'It feels as if that was a painful decision.'

Item 46: Try to 'cheer up' the patient.

When visiting the sick we may feel that part of our role is to make them 'feel better', either by telling funny stories or by getting them to 'look on the bright side and not be gloomy'. Perhaps the best comment on this item is that provided by Causley's fourth visitor:

> The fourth attempts to cheer
> His aged mother with light jokes
> Menacing as shell-splinters.
> 'They'll soon have you jumping round
> Like a gazelle,' he says.
> 'Playing in the football team.'
> Quite undeterred by the sight of kilos
> Of plaster, chains, lifting-gear,

A pair of lethally designed crutches,
'You'll be leap-frogging soon,' he says.
'Swimming ten lengths of the baths.'

At these unlikely prophecies
The old lady stares fearfully
At her sick, sick offspring
Thinking he has lost his reason—

Which, alas, seems to be the case.

(Causley, 1983)

Working through some of the items on this list might well create tensions and discomfort, as well as many laughs at the things that we say and do, but it is hoped that such tensions could be worked through in a creative way and thus strengthen the ministry of all concerned.

Other Schemes

A different way of visiting sick people who are hospitalized is for a group to 'adopt' a ward or unit within the hospital. It may be that the group is a local church who undertake to visit one ward on a regular basis and form a relationship with the patients and staff, in collaboration with the chaplaincy. This can work very well with the longer-stay units, such as those for the elderly sick, for the mentally ill or mentally handicapped. If such a relationship can be fostered, many things may become possible. In one hospital where I worked a local church 'adopted' a ward for mentally disturbed elderly people. A group from the church would visit once a month and spend time talking to the residents on the ward. It was not easy visiting, since some of the residents, at times, could be quite disturbed. Because the visitors came as a group they found it a little less threatening and it was clear that we needed to meet together with some of the staff every so often to try to understand why some of the residents behaved the way they did. This increased understanding and also increased confidence, and by the end of a year several things had developed. By arrangement with the staff some of the old people would be collected by church members and taken to their Wednesday afternoon club, to attend their Sunday service at the local church, to have a Christmas dinner with other elderly people from the local community, to go to a local pub for a drink. This latter activity was especially popular since many of the elderly patients had been used to evenings in the pub and had missed them once they became hospitalized. The mental state of several residents greatly improved with the introduction of such 'normal' social activities — providing medical clearance was obtained regarding the interaction of medication and alcohol. Occasionally a religious service would be conducted in the day rooom by the church members, but basically they were showing that the local church cared, that these people were loved and respected, that the staff were valued and this did not necessarily need to be expressed in 'churchy' language.

Gradually other groups began to 'adopt' units, including local infant and junior schools and the children would visit with their teachers and parents. The children would bring some of their art work and pin it up in the dayroom for the patients to enjoy after the visit, or they would perform part of a recent school concert. It was very moving to see an otherwise uncommunicative old lady suddenly having a very animated talk with an inquisitive seven-year-old. Since many of these wards were located in the former workhouse buildings, the scheme had the effect of bringing the community *into* the building and gradually eroding the stereotyped image that the community had about being 'admitted into that place'. Activities such as these can be undertaken by an individual church or a group of churches co-operating together. Since some people have a great aversion to hospital, or may themselves be physically unable to undertake visiting, it may be feasible for them to write letters to those in hospital or housebound, or to telephone them for a chat. It is helpful if those who write letters make it clear that they do not expect a reply, so that the receipt of several letters can be a source of pleasure and continuing care rather than become another burden for the sick person.

Whatever activity happens it can be a way of showing that God in the Church in the community is loving and caring and that it is a corporate activity of the whole Church and not just the responsibility of the individual minister. With the move at

government level to close many of our larger psychiatric
hospitals and create local community units many clergy may
feel very daunted, if not overwhelmed, at the prospect of
exercising pastoral care for such people without the real
backing and support of their congregations (see chapter 7).

Much of what has been said above in relation to 'chaplaincy
visitors' in hospitals can also be applied to church groups
undertaking pastoral care for sick people at home. There is
much scope for co-operation between adjacent schemes in
that it might be feasible to join together for training or for the
ongoing support groups. Those working in the hospital could
be a valuable resource to those visiting at home. Care would
be needed however not to overload those members of a
church who are 'chaplaincy visitors' by implying that they are
ideally suited to *also* undertake sick-visiting in the parish!
The same principle would apply to those health-care
professionals who live in the community. They *may* be very
willing on occasion to help in preparing pastoral visitors but
this should not be assumed and taken for granted.

The above schemes all focus on people who are already
sick, whether they be at home or in hospital. Although not
strictly the focus of this book there is also the preventive and
'health enhancing' aspect of the Church's ministry of healing.
This is perhaps seen clearly in such activities as bereavement
visiting as described by Dyne (1981), as undertaken by
Cruse (see Appendix A), or in projects such as the
Westminster Bereavement Project and Norfolk Bereavement
Care. Some of these projects are Church-based, others are
secular, but they all recruit, train and support voluntary
visitors who undertake to visit and offer support to the
bereaved. Since bereaved people are often more vulnerable to
illness, especially elderly people in the first year of
bereavement, such visiting schemes can fulfil a valuable
preventive function. In some instances, of course, the
bereavement visits are a continuation of the pastoral support
given to a family during the time of the terminal illness of the
person who has died. Thus the pastoral care of the sick can
have a preventive aspect in respect of the family of the sick
person in that the help and support they receive may prevent
them also becoming casualties. Many relatives of sick people
find travelling to and from hospital, the anxiety and

uncertainty about the future, having severely restricted freedom because of an elderly demented parent or sitting up at night with someone who is terminally ill all take their toll. In such circumstances the role of the church might well be to support the family and offer relief as necessary rather than going to the hospital to visit the one who is sick.

SEVEN

Some Specific Visiting Situations

Within this chapter we shall look at some of the pastoral considerations that it is helpful to be aware of in a selection of specific situations. The chapter does not seek to be exhaustive of all specialties, nor of all the issues that might arise in any particular specialty, but to provide some prompts which, it is hoped, will help to create a sensitivity to facets of pastoral care that might otherwise be missed.

The Surgical Patient

An acute surgical ward is usually a very busy place, and the pastoral visitor will encounter people who are waiting for, or have had, a wide variety of operations. The prospect of surgery is not something that is usually welcomed by people even when the necessity for it is acknowledged. During the course of our growth and development we establish an image of our selves and our bodies and of the way we interact with other people. We attach values to the various parts of our body in that some of them are more highly valued than others, some are more mentionable than others. What is important to most people is that that *body image* should not be disrupted and that we should remain intact. An interesting aspect of this is contained within Judaism in that the family of an orthodox Jew who dies following an operation necessitating amputation of a limb may well ask for the amputated limb to be returned so that it can be buried with the deceased. Similarly, following a post-mortem examination (usually only agreed to on medico-legal grounds), the relatives will insist on all organs and visceral fluids being returned for burial with the body. Surgery can represent a major disruption of our body image, and patients will sometimes describe the experience as one of being 'invaded' or 'mutilated'.

When visiting surgical patients it is tempting to grade the severity of the operation in accordance with our own experience or valuation. Such assumptions may be wildly inaccurate and lead to inappropriate responses. The patient who has been admitted for a routine (elective) operation which is deemed to be of a minor nature may not perceive it as such himself. Because of the routine nature of operations such as tonsillectomy, appendicectomy, haemorrhoidectomy or hernia repairs, the fact that these are *not routine to the patient* may be overlooked by staff and by visitors. The traumatic effect of having one's body cut open by someone else is very strong for some patients, not only in the more obviously mutilating operations of limb amputation, mastectomy, or creation of a stoma but also in 'minor' elective surgery. It is important to attend to *our* assumptions and elicit from the patient what this experience means to them.

John had been troubled by a hernia for several years. From time to time it would cause great discomfort and pain but usually went back into place and he was able to carry on with life as usual. It was clear however that the only permanent solution was an operation. There was a long waiting list in his area but eventually his name came to the top of the list and he received a phone call to say that if he could get to the hospital by 10 a.m. the next morning he could have a bed. It was not the best time to be off work and it was getting near to the time of the holiday that he and his wife had booked months before. However, provided he was not cancelled, he would be home in good time to return to work for a few weeks prior to the holiday. John had never been into hospital before and so felt quite apprehensive. Once he had been admitted to the ward he was seen by the surgical registrar prior to the ward round. On examination he told John that the hernia was not too bad and perhaps they need not operate! At first John felt a fraud for being there, then daunted at the prospect of continuing with the truss, the pain and the discomfort which *could* be very disabling even if all seemed well at the moment. As all this raced through his mind he knew he had to speak up before he was discharged and went to the end of the waiting list again. He told the registrar what he was thinking and reinforced how the quality of his life could be very different when the hernia was bad, adding that the Professor had explained to John in the clinic that this was the only remedy. John was then 'put on the list' for Thursday.

Having, in effect, argued his own case for surgery John now felt even more apprehensive. He was sent down for X-ray, ECG (electrocardiograph) to check his heart, and blood tests, returning to the ward in time for the doctor's round. On arrival at his bedside the Professor looked at John's notes, examined John and said, 'It's not bad at the moment but we'll sort it out on Thursday for you, then you'll have no more trouble. It's very routine. Soon have you up and about again. You could be home at the weekend.' Then he passed to the next patient. Whilst John felt vindicated in sticking to his guns with the registrar he wasn't too sure about the 'home at the weekend' part of the Professor's visit. That evening he had several visitors, including his wife, who all reassured him that there 'was nothing to it' and, since they all saw it as so straightforward, it seemed childish to say he was scared. He was not frightened about dying but more with the fact that under the anaesthetic he would not be in control. John was a very self-contained and controlled person, and the prospect of handing over total control to other people made him uneasy. He was being invited to put complete trust in a group of strangers who could open him up and then do whatever they wanted while he was unconscious. He knew this was irrational and that there were clear limits to what they could do in theatre, but this was the first time he had had to surrender himself in such a way and he was very anxious.

The arrival of the anaesthetist to examine John and obtain consent was very important in that she explained the operation and checked that John understood. Then she explained that her role was to anaesthetize John and to monitor his body systems and to look after him entirely while he was in theatre. She asked him how he was feeling and in response to his fears she reassured him that he was not being silly and that, whilst it would not be necessary with his operation, she did have the power to stop an operation at any point if she felt it in the patient's best interest to do so. John felt more able to contain his anxiety after this discussion and had a reasonable night's sleep. The operation *was* straightforward and on his return to the ward John was given good analgesic cover to monitor his pain and he felt quite comfortable. There was a sense of unreality in that he was not sure whether he had had an operation at first and so when the ward sister came to get him out of bed he readily complied—until he got his legs over the side of the bed. It was then that he realized his abdomen had been cut. With the encouragement of the sister he made it to the nearby chair although he was almost bent double as he shuffled across the floor. However, he managed. That first day was a haze with feelings of nausea from the anaesthetic, a headache and pain as the analgesia wore off. At visiting time he felt very tired but tried to be bright, without much success, and was glad when the other visitors left and his wife just sat quietly by the bedside. Night sedation ensured a good night's sleep and he felt a bit stronger the next day.

Walking to the treatment room and having his dressing changed almost finished him and even the rest on the bed did not prepare him for the next shock. When the doctor's round reached his bed he *was told* how well he was doing and that he could go home the next day; the district nurse would be in to see to the dressings and take the stitches out. He would be given an appointment to return to the clinic at a later date. Part of him felt relieved in that he would be able to go away on holiday as arranged, he knew there was a great pressure for beds and that his operation had been successful. Yet at the same time he felt unprepared to go home and was worried about how he would cope, since he did not feel sufficiently independent at this stage. John subsequently described how vulnerable and dependent he felt when he arrived home. He was afraid of bursting his wound and having no one there who could repair it. He also found he was quite childlike in his needs and emotional responses. He needed time to make the transition from illness to wellness and his rehabilitation was greatly helped by the understanding and the valuing of his feelings by his wife and the district nurse.

There will be many patients like John who have been admitted for 'minor' surgery as well as those who are in for large surgical operations and who may not be sure about the outcome of their operation. Just as John had to sort out whether or not he could safely entrust himself to others, so other patients will be trying to decide whether they can trust the information they have been given concerning their illness and their future. Some people will be facing the need to adjust to the loss of a body part which has inevitably affected their body image and initiated a grief reaction for what they used to be. This grief reaction may be overlaid by a fear of malignancy and/or relief that the growth or tumour has been removed. Nevertheless, the fact that you are no longer as physically complete as you were when you entered hospital does mean that you must adjust to a new image of yourself and perhaps a new way of relating to other people. For example the lady who has had a mastectomy may be relieved that the malignancy has been removed but also anxious about how she and her partner will relate to each other now that she is physically different. One cannot assume a value for what has been lost since it will vary from person to person (see Speck, 1978). It is important pastorally to find out from the patient what this event means to them. Frequently a loss of one part of the body links to other losses which are consequential. Thus the person who has an arm amputated following an accident may lose more than the arm itself, in that the amputation may affect the ability to drive, to enjoy recreational activities, to work—with consequent loss of earnings, etc. In some ways the loss of the limb may be the least important part for the patient, at least at the time when we are visiting. It is frequently the family, the GP and those offering pastoral care in the community who will see and become involved with the long-term effects of such surgery. The parallel between grief following bereavement and the grief reaction following surgical loss is well documented and indicates a similar time-scale for making an adjustment, so that people may require one or two years before they have formed a new and more acceptable body image. The continuing support of family and friends is a vital part of such rehabilitation, or the availability of a supportive group where there is no family.

Visiting people before and after an operation requires a sensitivity to the anxieties which the sick person may have and therefore a readiness to listen to any apprehension and fear without being too quick to offer blanket reassurance. The pastoral visitor may also feel apprehensive about what may be seen—the drips, the blood transfusion, the catheter bag, the surgical wound, the stoma, the nasogastric tube (a tube from the stomach draining via the nose into a bag). It is sometimes difficult to see the person behind all the hardware, but if we *can* focus on the person much of our anxiety about the attachments may be overcome and allow us to be attentive to the patient rather than our own feelings. It is not always easy, especially if the patient takes a delight in giving us all the gory details, showing us the scars, or responding in an unexpected way. One week after I commenced work as a hospital chaplain I visited a very frightened elderly lady who was awaiting an operation. Feeling it important to encourage her to talk about the operation I stayed some time and then suggested we said some prayers and I gave her a blessing. I felt I had done a reasonable job with my first surgical patient and promised to visit after the operation. When I returned I found her looking rather weak and frail but she seemed pleased to see me. I felt in control of the situation and not unduly worried by the tubes attached to her. I sat on the edge of the bed, being careful *not* to sit on the catheter, and held her hand. Then she placed her other hand on my shoulder and pulled me towards her. I overbalanced and ended up spread-eagled across the patient. As I scrambled up I heard laughter behind me and turning round saw that the consultant and his team had arrived and witnessed the incident. His only comment before moving down the ward was 'I presume this is total patient care, Padre?'

The Medical Patient

Medical patients tend to be classed as either acute or chronic depending on the nature of their illness. Many of those who are visited at home by pastoral visitors tend to be the chronic sick, who are frequently also elderly and housebound. From time to time such people may need admission to hospital because their condition has deteriorated or their medication needs adjusting. It may be that they have developed some secondary problem or a new treatment has become available and the consultant has suggested, on one of their many out-patient appointments, that it might be suitable for them. Thus the patient who is disabled with arthritis may be admitted for a short while for a course of injections and physiotherapy to try to mobilize some very stiff joints. The person with diabetes may be admitted to hospital at regular intervals until the diabetes has been stabilized, but otherwise may be maintained at home with the support of the GP and the community nursing service. Similarly the person with chronic chest disease may require regular readmission to hospital, especially in the winter months, in addition to having bottled oxygen and drug treatment at home. In such situations the focus for pastoral care may well be that of on-going support over a period of many years, perhaps encouraging as full a life as possible for as long as possible. In some cases the pastor may become involved in supportive counselling, as the sick person adjusts to another loss consequent on the illness which has disabled them further. In the case of disseminated sclerosis or *myaesthenia gravis* the patient may be quite well for long periods and then begin to deteriorate and fear that the disease is taking over and may disable them more. Setting realistic goals can be very important in such situations, so that the person does not become discouraged by failure but remains 'in control' of their environment and their achievements. Readmission to hospital also needs to be seen as a way of regaining control over the illness rather than symptomatic of defeat. As with the loss resulting from surgery, so in the case of medical conditions the patient may experience a variety of losses over a period of years and spend much of their life living with uncertainty as to what their future will be.

The greater emphasis in orthodox medicine towards home treatment programmes means that some people will be in charge of their own treatment as, for example, people with haemophilia who will have a 'home treatment pack' to give themselves the Factor VIII clotting factor to save them from having to attend the hospital each day. Many of these people can also manage their own care in the case of a bleed, and therefore are much more in control of their own bodies and lifestyle. Those who care for the sick in the community may meet people who are at home for most of the time and only visit the hospital for specific treatment and care on an out-patient basis. People who are receiving chemotherapy or radiotherapy treatment at the hospital may do so on an out-patient basis or with a short overnight admission. Since, on their return home, they may experience nausea and tiredness and therefore not be very communicative, it may be much better to visit a few days after treatment. Good liaison between the family, the sick person and the pastoral visitor is obviously important if a sensitive relationship of trust is to develop.

Another example of home treatment is the person with kidney failure who may well be dialysing at home. This usually means that one room of the house has been set up solely for dialysis and the person will dialyse in that room for several hours a week, either overnight or during the day. Visits need to be by arrangement, since the times when the person is going on to the machine or coming off are not good times to visit. However, once on the machine the time can be quite boring and visits may be much appreciated—provided the visitor can cope with the sight of blood being pumped out of and back into the body via the artificial kidney machine. In addition to the needs of the person who is dialysing, consideration must be given to the pastoral care of the family. Not all families find it easy to cope with home dialysis, and whilst some will assist the person to dialyse others will keep well away—or be told to stay away by the patient. Being tied to a machine three or more times a week can create quite a strain for some families in spite of a good supportive network at the local renal unit.

Many of the chronic sick in hospital and at home tend to be elderly, though clearly not all old people are sick. It has been estimated that by the year 2000 some 80 per cent of hospital beds will be occupied by people over sixty-five years of age. Admission to hospital and removal from their home can create great confusion in addition to any confusion already created by the illness. A difficult aspect of ageing is the way in which recent memory deteriorates whilst past memories seem sharper. This means that they may become unsure about time and place and need people to remind them and give them time to respond to questions and requests. Sight and hearing may also be affected, whether because of cataracts or increasing deafness (the extent of which may be difficult to assess until you say something you don't wish them to hear). These disabilities may create frustrations and lead to irritableness.

The diseases of old age add to the frustrations of the normal ageing process, so that some formerly active elderly people may have to readjust to a new lifestyle because of a stroke, osteoarthritis, breaking a limb, Parkinson's disease or cancer. With good family and community care such people may be able to remain in their own home, but with the changing pattern of family life such support may not always be available. Admission to hospital may, therefore, carry with it an associated and very real fear of never returning home again, a fear which can make some elderly people reluctant to seek medical help unless it is a dire emergency. If residential care does become necessary, a home visit prior to transfer may enable the elderly person to say 'goodbye' to the family home which can be a cause of great grief. It is important when visiting sick elderly people to introduce oneself clearly, to speak slowly and to sit in a position where the person can see you clearly without having to painfully raise their head because you are standing above them. An important aspect of pastoral care with the elderly is to offer reassurance, enhance confidence and to instil the feeling that they are not forgotten or abandoned by us, the Church, or God. This is in addition to all that has been said earlier concerning communication, inadequacy and fear (chapter 5). Patience on the part of the visitor is also important; so too is the ability not to outstay one's welcome. Whilst visiting a group of elderly patients I introduced myself to one of them. 'I'm deaf,' she said. So I repeated my introduction a little louder and clearer. 'I still can't hear, I need my hearing aid.' This was found in the locker and fitted and I reintroduced myself. 'Well I'm a Catholic,' she replied and promptly removed her hearing aid and put it back in the locker! Remembering that sick people are a captive audience and the importance of not abusing our right of access to patients by outstaying our welcome is another vital part of pastoral care.

The Infectious Patient — AIDS, Hepatitis B+

Some hospital medical wards will include patients with

infectious diseases such as hepatitis B+, HIV+ (AIDS), and some resistant infections that necessitate the patient being isolated for a while. There are always clear labels on the doors of these rooms to indicate the nature of the protection, as explained earlier (chapter 4). Many patients who are barrier-nursed feel very isolated and welcome visitors. However, the permission of the ward staff *must always be sought before entering the patient's room.* Provided the relevant precautions are taken regarding the protective clothing provided and hand washing there is no reason why a pastoral visitor should be at risk from visits, whether they be purely social or to administer the sacraments. (See pp. 44 — 5 for discussion of administration of sacraments to people who are being barrier-nursed.)

The feeling of stigmatization, together with the anxiety about their illness, can make such patients very frightened. Some people may feel angry that they have acquired an infection through no fault of their own and it may seem to them, and to us, very unfair. Others may be very aware of their own part in becoming infected, may be blaming themselves for what has happened, and also be anxious about other people with whom they have been in contact. In respect of AIDS the need to respond in a sensitive and non-judgemental way to the person who is in need is paramount, irrespective of how they have acquired the virus, as behoves good pastoral care. The guidelines issued by the Church of England's Board of Social Responsibility (BSR) underline the importance of a sensitive approach on the part of the pastor:

> Pastors need to ask similar questions about their own attitudes to questions of sexual orientation and practice, and addiction. The bedside of a gay AIDS patient is not the place for the pastor to be working out his or her anxieties about sexuality; this needs to be done elsewhere. Pastors should ask themselves these questions: 'Can I detect in myself a tendency to view haemophiliac AIDS sufferers as more sadly affected than gay men or drug-users with the disease?', 'Do I find in myself more compassion for the "innocent" recipient of contaminated blood products, than for those whose infection may have been as a result of illegal drug use or sexual activity?' Whatever the pastor's

view of the morality of differing lifestyles, the prime responsibility is not to obtain agreement on the boundaries of acceptable behaviours, but to reveal God's love for and valuing of each individual. (BSR, 1986)

It can also be important to liaise with others who are supporting/counselling, so that communication between the patient and others involved is clear. A good accepting pastoral relationship at an early stage can enable a more meaningful ministry if the patient enters the terminal stage of his or her life. If, as pastors, we find our anxieties about such visits prevent us from visiting, it is better to acknowledge this and discuss it with ward staff, or the staff who advise the hospital about such matters (i.e. control of infection nurse or microbiologist). We may then need to discuss it with other members of the pastoral care team to see if another member feels able to take on this task rather than deny the patient access to pastoral care.

Maternity and Gynaecology Visits

One of the criticisms of modern orthodox medicine is the way in which it tends to medicalize natural life-events such as childbirth. The Natural Childbirth Trust and other such bodies have sought to challenge this over-medicalization and to restore more choice about the method and the place where a mother gives birth. If we are visiting a maternity department, whether a small GP unit or a larger hospital unit, it is important to remind ourselves that the women we shall meet are fit and well and pregnant. Therefore, such visits can often be very relaxed and enjoyable. Only a very small percentage will have any ill health in addition to their pregnancy. If they have been admitted some time before delivery, because of high blood pressure or a threat to lose the child, they may be very bored with bedrest and anxious about the baby. If the mother has been delivered and all is well it is not always easy to find the most convenient time to visit, as the mother may be resting, doing post-natal exercises with the physiotherapist, or feeding the child.

Male pastoral visitors may sometimes find it embarrassing to visit the maternity department because they do not know what to say to the expectant mother or the new mother and baby. It is always easier to visit when one has a clear role to perform or something to take to the person visited and this is very true with the maternity department. Seeing a chaplain on the maternity unit can be a visible reminder of the link between the creativity of parenthood and the creative power of God, leading to thoughts about baptism, thanksgiving and communion. It is significant that the major religions of the world have each evolved appropriate 'rites of passage' in connection with the various normal life crises that people experience, of which childbirth is one. The multicultural nature of the hospital community in many areas may mean that more people may wish to arrange for circumcision than for 'churching' or baptism. However, as Wesley Carr (1985) has indicated so clearly, the occasional offices can provide us with very important pastoral opportunities to relate to a family in a way that enables them to discover the relevance and the nearness of God throughout their life. Since many of the women on a maternity ward will be up and about the ward, it is not too difficult for those who wish to attend the chapel or a service in the dayroom, whether that be a service of thanksgiving or for holy communion.

A sense of humour can be a great asset in all pastoral care and not least in a maternity department where emotions may be quite labile. A young woman was admitted to hospital on account of high blood pressure associated with her pregnancy. After a few days she was told that she was carrying twins and would need to stay in hospital until delivered. She was a communicant member of the Church of England and established a good rapport with the chaplain. When the obstetricians informed her that the latest scan showed that it was triplets and not twins she was very upset and anxious about how she and her husband would be able to cope with three babies at the same time. By this time her abdomen had also grown considerably and was very uncomfortable. On the Sunday morning she met with the chaplain in the sister's office for the communion service. Because of her size she was unable to sit down and decided to stand with her large bulge propped on the desk to relieve the weight. She was still very tearful and tense at the beginning of the service. When the chaplain reached the words, 'Come unto me all ye who labour, and I will give you rest,' there was a moment's silence and then both began to laugh and had great difficulty in regaining control. Far from being irreverent the laughter transformed the situation and, after receiving the sacrament, the mother-to-be was noticeably calmer and more relaxed.

The short length of time that most people stay on a maternity ward means that there is a rapid 'turn-over' which makes it very difficult to meet, let alone minister pastorally, to many of those giving birth. Rather than ignore the unit because of this difficulty it may be best to focus on good staff contact so that they know the people who are available pastorally, what they may be able to offer, and thus make more appropriate referrals for pastoral care. In addition to the rapid 'turn-over' the completeness of the mother and baby pair can make pastoral visitors feel that they are intruding, or that they are uninitiated members of the group and therefore have no right to be there. This sense of being shut out can create embarrassment, not only for the male visitor but also for some women pastors who may find the image of the nursing mother creates feelings within themselves which either draw them in or seem to push them away.

The same feeling, or message of completeness, can be experienced by the midwife who also has the requirement to instruct and support the new mother and child. The desire of the mother to 'get home quickly and establish my own routine' can sometimes reflect an ambivalence within the mother regarding the need for help and guidance, and the desire to be self-sufficient and have 'my baby to myself'. The father may also have mixed feelings about the birth (apart from whether or not he should be present at the delivery) in that once the baby is born he may find it difficult to relate to a seemingly unresponsive child who is not bonded to 'Dad'. This may lead to a resentment of the amount of time that the mother has to spend with the baby by the father and by other children in the family which, because they recognize it is irrational, may create a sense of guilt.

The time following the birth of a baby can be emotionally turbulent for the mother. The joy which follows the safe delivery of the baby may give way to tears and anxiety. The mother may find that she is unable to articulate any reason for this, so adding to her distress. This may, in part, be related to a sense of mourning for the loss of herself as she was before she became a mother. Such reactions are most commonly experienced several days after the birth and are usually associated with the time when the mother's milk comes into her breasts. The mother's hormone levels take some time to stabilize after childbirth and so she is more vulnerable to rapid changes of mood at this time. This can be very disconcerting for her partner who may find that, at times, whatever he says or does is 'wrong'. The demands of the baby, coupled with the child's total dependence upon the parent, can easily lead to physical exhaustion and anger at the baby's seeming unwillingness to learn and accept the mother's routine. This can create a sense of guilt since the parents also know that such expectations are unrealistic. The support and knowledge of the midwifery staff and others can enable most parents to work through this period of adjustment without any adverse effects.

For some mothers the 'baby blues' persist and may lead to the development of a full depressive illness (post-puerperal depression) for which medical intervention may be necessary. This is usually recognized in those mothers who are known to be predisposed to depressive illness or where the above common reactions do not ease and may persist for many weeks. This can render the mother unable to care properly for the baby and, in extreme cases, can also increase the risk of harm to the child (see Kitzinger, 1977, ch. 22).

Occasionally all is not well with the newborn baby and he/she may need to be admitted to the special care baby unit (SCBU) either in the same hospital or a neighbouring hospital. If the baby's life is threatened by prematurity, illness or abnormality, the parents may request baptism, as mentioned earlier. Sometimes the life of the child will be affected before or during birth so that the child may die in the womb (described as an intra-uterine death), be miscarried (as a spontaneous abortion before 28 weeks gestation), or stillborn (if after 28 weeks gestation). In such situations it is important to consider the pastoral needs of the staff as well as the parents. It is also important to recognize that we, as chaplain or pastoral visitor, may also require support which may come from the staff group or on occasions may be offered by the 'patient'.

The supportive care that the 'patient' may give to the 'carer' was illustrated very movingly for me one day when I was called to the labour ward to visit a lady who, eighteen months before, had suffered the death of a young child in a tragic accident. I had ministered to the family at that time and shared much of their pain and grief. The mother was now in the labour ward awaiting the delivery of her next child by caesarian section. Her husband was to be present since she would be having an epidural anaesthetic and therefore would be awake, and she told the obstetrician she also wanted the chaplain to be there. He thought this an odd request but bleeped the chaplain who went to the ward, changed, and then went with them into theatre—albeit apprehensively. During the operation the mother told the surgeon that 'the chaplain was with us eighteen months ago when we had so much pain and so we wanted him here today to share in our joy'. Shortly afterwards she was delivered of a fine healthy girl and the joy was shared by all.

Gynaecology wards can also present difficulties for pastoral visitors and yet can be very rewarding. The patients on a gynaecology ward will include women who have come for an abortion or are being investigated because of infertility, those with a variety of problems relating to the menstrual cycle, those awaiting a hysterectomy or being investigated following an abnormal cervical smear or the discovery of an abdominal mass of unknown origin. For some women it will be simple surgery with a very short stay in hospital and a complete recovery of health. Others will have all the problems of uncertainty of diagnosis and their future following the discovery of a malignancy and the need for chemotherapy or radiotherapy treatment. Those who have had a hysterectomy or sterilization, or have discovered that their infertility cannot be corrected, may need support in adjusting to loss. The important aspect of pastoral care in such situations of loss is to be attentive to the assumptions we make about the value of what has been lost by the patient. Some people will be relieved to have a hysterectomy, others will find it very upsetting. By sensitively listening to what the person has to say we can discover what this experience means to them and so respond more sensitively and appropriately. Because of the personal nature of many of these conditions the chaplain/

visitor may experience a certain amount of 'testing out' to determine how shockable or down to earth they are before feelings and reactions are shared.

The Paediatric Patient

The child patient is not a mini-adult but a person in his or her own right and, whilst it is helpful to have some understanding of the developmental stages in a child's life, allowance must be made for the fact that people do regress when they are ill. Therefore a fourteen-year-old may behave more like an eleven-year-old *at times* because of the artificial, and at times frightening, situation in which he finds himself. Open visiting makes quite a difference to many wards, together with the provision of parent-and-child rooms. Depending on the developmental stages of the child there may be a variety of anxieties, fears and stresses, some of which are real and others which are in the child's fantasy. Watching what happens to other children on the ward, together with previous experience of hospital, can either allay or enhance these fears. It is, therefore, important to be truthful with the child. Thus to say that an injection will not hurt, when it usually does, can quickly erode trust. The importance of carefully preparing the child for any unpleasant or painful experience is one of the items referred to by Burton (1975, p. 100f.) and Autton's excellent book on pain (1986, ch. 4). Children recognize and respond to genuineness and are very quick to spot those who are genuinely interested and concerned. Separation anxieties can be very evident with some children, especially if the child is a long way away from home or school and so unable to be visited frequently. Illnesses which require treatment in a major centre in another part of the country can create this problem, plus feelings of guilt in the parents if there are other children in the family, since they feel torn as to where they should be at any time.

Play is a very good entrée into the world of the child, especially at times of sickness. The way in which a child plays a game or draws pictures can indicate an 'acting out' of his or her feelings. Many hospitals have a school attached to the paediatric department and the teachers, who seek to continue the child's normal education whilst in hospital, can be a great help to the pastor in seeking to understand the world-view of the child in hospital. Additionally the teachers may also value the support of the chaplain/pastor in helping them to cope with their feelings and reactions concerning some of the children they teach who may be terminally ill. With the dying child the teachers may sometimes find themselves caught between the child and the parents. The child and parent may be protecting each other from discussing the truth of the situation and the child may therefore share feelings with the teacher (or pastor). If the parents feel that the teacher has a closer relationship with the child than their own they may resent this and become critical of the appropriateness of education at such a time in the child's life. Some children find the sense of 'normality', which the visit of the teacher signifies, can be very reassuring, even if the child knows that he or she may not make it to the final examination. In addition it must be recognized that the education provided may be on a very broad base and, on occasion, may be education for dying. The needs of the other children in a family should not be overlooked, especially in respect of sibling rivalry, which may feed ideas that a brother or sister is ill because of rivalrous feelings within the other child.

The staff on a paediatric unit may also experience emotional strain and look to the pastor as a means of support. As with the obstetric unit, a pastor may not always find it easy to 'get into' the paediatric unit in that staff may seem slightly possessive of 'my children'. However, a readiness to be called in at any time in addition to general visits to the staff on the unit can help them feel more able to share their frustrations and feelings of inadequacy with the pastor. Within the community the pastor may not have the same opportunity to meet with the medical and nursing staff who are visiting the home of the sick child. It may, however, be possible to establish a link with the General Practitioner and staff of the health centre which could enable a mutually supportive relationship to develop.

The Mentally Ill

Within the Library of Pastoral Care another volume has focused on the relationship between the pastor and the mentally ill (Foskett, 1984). In this work Foskett enables us to enter what at times can be a frightening world for both patient, family and helper. The search for meaning at a time of sickness is very evident in psychiatric illness but because of the difficulty of understanding what is being experienced by the sufferer it can seem very threatening to those outside of that experience. To find ways of relating to such people we need to gain some understanding of the various forms in which mental illness may present itself: viz. the psychoses, neuroses, anxiety states and depression. Foskett (1984) and Grainger (1979) help us to enter into this world and find ways of relating which can help us to function as pastors as distinct from the various therapists who may also be caring for the person.

It is often lack of understanding which feeds the anxieties of many people and which creates alarm at the thought of the large mental hospital being closed and patients transferred to smaller community units. This process of 'Sectorisation of Mental Health Services', in response to the DHSS policy of transition to community care, has implications for pastoral care whether provided by the local church or the officially appointed hospital chaplains. With this in mind Canon John Browning undertook some research into the 'Development of the Role of a Community Mental Health Chaplain' (submitted to the Trent Regional Health Authority). This work looked at ways in which the future pastoral needs of the mentally ill might be better met by a partnership between the local community church and a Community Mental Health Chaplain who could exercise a co-ordinating role.

John Browning's report indicates that there is already a good degree of involvement by local church groups in projects relating to rehabilitation and resettlement of mentally ill people. This is illustrated in a pilot project set up in Newcastle, and jointly funded by the health authority and the social services department, with a view to establishing the 'Newcastle Chaplaincy for Mental Health'. Their initial premise was that

> In the years to come more and more treatment for mental illness will be provided in the community rather than in hospital, and it will be to the local Christian Ministers,

rather than a specialist hospital chaplaincy, that sufferers will turn for spiritual help and counsel. The Newcastle Chaplaincy for Mental Health will in some instances offer such help directly to sufferers but in most instances the aim will be to equip and train Local Ministers and Lay Christians to perform this ministry themselves. (Browning, 1986, p. 17)

During the course of this project the prevalence of stigmatized attitudes, a need for education and training regarding the stereotypes of mental ill health and ways to develop more appropriate modes of pastoral care became apparent. In that many people will still need to be cared for within an institution, there will probably be much support for the interim view held in Newcastle that 'any future chaplaincy service to mental health in Newcastle must be *community based* while still continuing to provide a service to in-patient facilities'. This is especially relevant in the interim period while the larger institutions are closing down, since staff as well as patients feel very stressed and anxious about the changes that are happening. In several parts of the country, where there has been a decline in clergy numbers, there is real concern over the Church's ability to respond to this increased pastoral need and responsibility. Browning also points out the need expressed by experienced clergy for guidance on matters of mental illness and mental health, with easier access to the other professionals supported by the experienced whole-time chaplain.

The changes that are happening in the field of mental health have necessitated a review of the role of the officially appointed chaplains to an institution caring for large numbers of 'in-patients'. It is not possible at this stage to see what form of pastoral care will evolve in the future in respect of mental health care. However, it is clear that some form of partnership will need to develop, based on a mutual trust between hospital chaplains, community churches and those working within the community in a voluntary or professional capacity. Browning's proposal of the 'network concept', with tasks being shared amongst the members of a team 'in a manner consonant with a theology of diversity of gifts working for the one Body' (op. cit., p. 26), has much to commend it, not only in the area of mental health but in respect of the pastoral care of sick people in receipt of other types of care as well. The trust and mutual respect required by such an approach is, in part, related to an understanding of the structure of the Health Service and the way it provides care which is the subject of the next chapter.

EIGHT

Institutional and Community Structures

The time is right for theology to make its contribution, not in competition to that of other contributors, but as one perspective among many which all seek the truth. (Foskett, 1984, p. 167)

If theology *is* to make a relevant contribution to the truth it is important that those who engage in pastoral care understand the contribution being made by others, together with the Health Service structure as seen within the institution and the community.

Towards the end of the nineteenth century a young priest in a Midlands town visited the home of a woman whose child had recently died of cholera. He offered her words of consolation to which she responded by saying, 'I realize that I must bear this sorrow since it is God's will.' The priest retorted, 'Nonsense woman, it was not God who killed your daughter—it was the drains.' It was clear to this priest that the pastoral care of this grieving mother and her family also carried with it a need to impress upon those responsible for health care in that town the urgency of reconstructing the drainage system. This incident is somewhat reminiscent of that described in a novel by A. J. Cronin (1983 edn) in which two young doctors, Andrew Manson and Philip Denny, are working in a South Wales mining valley in the 1920s. They discovered that an outbreak of paratyphoid was linked to a faulty sewer and that the landowners were unwilling to replace it. The two doctors conspire to demolish the sewer themselves and, late one night, they float dynamite down the sewer and blow it up!
These two incidents illustrate that the provision of health

care, especially its preventive aspects, are inextricably linked with social and political issues and structures. Thus the passing of the Public Health Act of 1848 was of great importance in that it permitted local authorities to introduce a number of sanitary reforms. It is, however, a peculiar feature of English public health legislation that so many powers are permissive, not compulsory, which meant on this occasion that the more adventurous areas made great progress whilst other areas lagged far behind, with the results highlighted by Cronin and others. What the Public Health Act did establish, however, was the State's responsibility for securing *minimum* conditions of health for the people. Because of the unequal way in which this was developed, there was a clear need to co-ordinate the personal health services and establish them on a national basis. This led to the National Health Services Act of 1946.

This Act dealt with such questions as medical treatment (at home and in hospital), health care for mothers and children, the provision of drugs and appliances, and the establishment of health centres. The Act took for granted the existence of a central government department responsible for the service as a whole, an ordered and reasonably efficient system of local government with measures to ensure a sufficiently healthy environment, i.e. a good supply of clean water, an efficient method of sewage disposal and of cleansing and draining the streets.

On the 5 July 1948 the Act became operative together with the recognition and provision that the spiritual needs of sick people should be catered for. This has led to the appointment and development of a hospital chaplaincy service, on either a whole-time or part-time basis, to the various health authorities throughout the country. Many of the asylums and larger mental institutions which preceded the 1946 Act already had officially appointed chaplains who cared for the spiritual needs of the patients. History frequently repeats itself and one can foresee the possibility of the history of public health being repeated in respect of the criteria for the appointment of hospital chaplains. The DHSS has not made the new criteria mandatory for health authorities but instead has said that:

The decision as to whether the appointment of a hospital chaplain is appropriate is a matter for the health authority . . . The Joint Committee for Hospital Chaplaincy has produced advisory notes on the criteria for the appointment for hospital chaplains. While these guidelines are in no way binding, health authorities reviewing their chaplaincy needs will find it helpful to be aware of them. (DHSS, PM[86]4.2)

Whilst it is good that health authorities should have the freedom to respond to local need, within the broader framework of a national guideline, nevertheless they can ignore these guidelines and go their own way, thus creating the possibility of an uneven development of chaplaincy within the NHS.

Just as the provision of health care is wider than meeting the needs of one sick person, so pastoral care is often broader than responding to the needs of that one individual. In many situations it is equally important to consider the influences which come to bear upon those offering care to that sick person—'Who cares for the carer?'—not least those in a professional role. In the area of hospital chaplaincy it is important to consider the *nature and impact* of the institution which cares for those who are sick on everyone involved whether at home or in hospital. This fact is also reflected in the new 'Criteria for Appointment' of hospital chaplains which state that 'Chaplains and chaplains' assistants should be appointed to the *whole* institution, to care pastorally for both patients and staff' (*Handbook on Hospital Chaplaincy*, 1987). It is, therefore, important that chaplains and others who visit the sick should have some understanding of the structure of the National Health Service and the pressures upon many of those within it. This will not only assist their direct ministry to the sick person but may also have an indirect effect upon the patient through offering help and appropriate support to the carer. (See chapter 10.)

The National Health Service has undergone a great many changes since it came into being in 1948. There was a major reorganization in 1968, a further one in 1974, a restructuring in 1982 and most recently the Griffiths Report (1983) which included changes intended to improve the management of hospitals and community services not least in terms of 'cost effectiveness'. At the time of writing, the Griffiths Report is now being implemented, together with an attempt to tackle the tension between clinical autonomy/infinite demands and finite resources. The National Health Service is expected to improve the management of the service and the efficiency with which services are delivered. In addition it is also expected, in the future, to generate much of the extra resources that will be needed by its own efforts. Whilst some would agree that there needs to be some reform along these lines there is, nevertheless, a great deal of uncertainty, stress and demoralization in certain sectors of the Health Service which can have an impact on the care given to those who are sick. In this sense the institution itself may become in need of pastoral care from those who visit it or work within it, lest it too become sick.

Structure of the NHS in England*

The Secretary of State at the *Department Of Health and Social Security* (*DHSS*) supervises the NHS, Personal Social Services and Social Security. In respect of the NHS the department allocates resources, makes policy and issues advice. A big issue currently, and for the foreseeable future, is that of finance, because the health service has to compete for funding from central government. The money obtained by the DHSS from the annual Public Expenditure Survey has then to be allocated to the next tier of the structure—the fourteen *Regional Health Authorities* (*RHA*). Because of

* The Health Service structure referred to here relates mainly to England. There are differences in the rest of the UK. In England the DHSS relates to a regional tier, but Scotland, Wales and Northern Ireland each have government departments which also fulfil some regional responsibility. These are known as the Scottish Home and Health Department; the Welsh Office; and the Department of Health and Social Security (Northern Ireland). Scotland has 15 Health Boards, and it is the primary care division of each Health Board which arranges the contracts with GPs, dentists, opticians and pharmacists. Wales has nine health authorities similar to England, and each has a Family Practitioner Committee. Northern Ireland has four Health and Social Services Boards which hold the contracts for GPs etc. through a Central Services Agency.

uneven distribution of funds to various parts of the country, the Resource Allocation Working Party (RAWP, 1976) produced a means of establishing targets for each authority and funding accordingly. This has resulted in some Regions receiving less now than in the past, in order that other parts of the country might benefit. In some parts of the country, notably London, it is claimed that RAWP has added to the impact of the present financial constraints.

The next tier in the NHS is the *District Health Authority* (*DHA*) of which there are 192. Within the District there will usually be one or more *Units* which may be a large single hospital; all community services; a group of smaller hospitals or mental illness/mental handicap services.

At each level or tier, following the Griffiths Report, there will be a General Manager (as opposed to the previous role of Administrator) who will have personal responsibility for the service delivered and the cost effectiveness of it. It is also envisaged that the medical staff should also exercise some responsibility for the budget by themselves becoming budget holders rather than other people's budgets being used to fund clinical practice.

The Hospital

Within the hospital itself there will be a variety of management structures as decided by the District and Unit General Managers and approved by the higher levels of management. Each department within the hospital will, as now, have its own departmental manager who will represent that department at the meetings for departmental managers. In addition there will be full representation of staff issues through the professional organizations and trade unions. Numerically the NHS is one of the largest employers within the UK, having over 1 million people on its payroll. Over 40 per cent of them are nurses and midwives. Other staff include: administrative and clerical; ambulance staff; ancillary (domestic, kitchens, laundry, portering); chaplains; doctors; professional and technical (laboratory, x-ray technicians, etc.); telephonists; therapists; works and maintenance; and others.

The picture is further complicated by the fact that in 1948 the British Medical Association resisted a state health service.

Therefore, GPs, dentists, pharmacists and opticians are not employed by the NHS, but are self-employed. Their contracts for the time they work within the NHS are administered by *Family Practitioner Committees (FPC)*.

The other group which seeks to influence decision making and monitor those providing health care is the Community Health Council, which usually relates to the District Health Authority. The CHC seeks to represent the interests of the public and each CHC must include local authority and voluntary organization members. Health authority employees cannot also be on the CHC within their own district. The CHC is not only concerned with complaints from the public but will also make suggestions to the authority about various schemes which might be considered to improve the service.

In order that clergy may relate more easily to the ward situation it is helpful to know something of the medical and nursing structure:

Medical

At the apex of the pyramid are the *Consultants* who are in charge of all medical work within the hospital, through the Medical Executive Council (MEC). All patients referred to hospital as in-patients or out-patients become the responsibility of the consultant. Next in line of responsibility are the *Senior Registrar* and *Registrar* who in turn supervise the work of the *Senior House Officer/House Officer* (usually referred to as 'houseman'). Together these constitute a 'firm' to which, in a teaching hospital, a number of medical students will be attached. Additionally, teaching hospitals will have a number of academic departments with medical staff attached to the university. These staff will divide their time between the NHS and research/teaching. Whilst not every patient will see the consultant responsible for their care, it is usual for there to be a consultant's ward round at least once a week, when all patients are reviewed by the firm, the ward staff and *relevant* other staff. These might include the physiotherapist, social worker, dietitian, and sometimes the chaplain. The chaplain is not automatically included in such ward rounds or in case conferences, and the onus is on the individual chaplain to show that he/she has a contribution to make and thus earns a place in that team. Similarly, because one is included in the membership of one ward team it does not follow that one will therefore automatically be a member of every other team in the hospital. In fact, on a practical level, such membership of every team would leave little time to actually see the patients whom one was meeting to discuss!

The ward round can sometimes be a daunting experience for the patient, especially if there is a large entourage, which may make it difficult to answer let alone ask questions. It can be helpful to suggest that the patient writes down any questions they may have for the doctor, so that they may be more able to ask them during the round—or ask to see the doctor afterwards. Frequently patients in teaching hospitals will be interviewed and examined by medical students as a vital part of the student's medical education. If, however, a patient finds this distressing they may decline but should make their wishes known to the medical/nursing staff as soon after admission as possible.

Nursing

The term 'Matron' is now rarely used in NHS hospitals since the Salmon report of 1963 which restructured nurse management. There is some variation in the title for the senior nurse manager which may be *Chief Nursing Officer* or *Director of Nursing Services* (*DNS*). There may then be *Divisional* and *Senior Nursing Officers* with responsibility for various sections of the nursing service who will act as line managers to the *Nursing Officers* who are in charge of units. (A unit may be three or more medical or surgical wards, a suite of operating theatres, or an accident and emergency department.) The Nursing Officers are a little closer to the patients though their actual involvement varies greatly. The actual ward is managed by the *ward sister* (female) or the *charge nurse* (male) who will be assisted by one or more staff nurses and student nurses.

Each discipline within the hospital will have its own professional structure, whether that be the medical staff or the works department. In some hospitals there may be various taboos and territorial boundaries across which other disciplines may not cross. It is interesting to note that the chaplain is one of the few people who has a virtual open access across all the disciplines in that he/she can usually turn up in various places without causing too much of a stir. This privilege of access is one to be safeguarded as a most valuable asset to the exercising of pastoral care within hospitals. In order to make the most of this freedom the chaplain must be familiar with the structure and set-up within the hospital where he/she works or visits. Credibility and trust are not ours 'as of right' but must be earned, and in many cases this may entail taking a longer time-scale before expecting things to happen. At the same time one must not be slow to make the most of the opportunities which are presented to us to build such a relationship of trust with staff. In one hospital a nurse complained about clergy visiting: 'They breeze in. Don't say a word to us.' Thus, when visiting a patient in hospital as a clergyman, it is important to introduce oneself to the ward staff and give some indication of your involvement with the patient. Apart from the obvious courtesy, knowing that a patient has a link with a local church can be an important piece of information in many cases.

The senior nurse on any ward has some responsibility to monitor, and in some instances restrict, who has access to patients. This is particularly important when one remembers the vulnerability and 'captive audience' aspect of being a patient. Whilst a 'dog collar' will open many doors and elicits much goodwill from hospital staff, there may still be occasions when staff may request no visitors. More will be gained by discussing the reasons with the nurse in charge than by insisting on rights of access. Similarly, complying with a request to 'only stay a few minutes' will greatly facilitate access on subsequent occasions rather than outstaying one's welcome and over-taxing the patient's strength. This applies equally to home visits, where the next of kin may make requests similar to those made by hospital staff.

The importance of being vigilant and checking with ward staff *before* visiting is especially clear in relation to patients who are being 'barrier nursed'. This may be either because the patient has an infectious disease which may be transmitted to visitors or other patients, or the patient's resistance to infection may be so low that she or he may need to be protected from other people and any infections they may have. An example of this would be a person being treated for leukaemia and who has had total body irradiation prior to bone-marrow transplantation. The patient's immune system is unable at this stage to combat infection, and so visiting is closely monitored and restricted. Staff would wish to minimize the isolating effect of such treatment and therefore would probably allow a pastoral visit, provided the visitor did not have a cold or a sore throat. It would also be necessary for the visitor to wear a face mask, apron/gown and disposable gloves. The fact that a patient is being barrier nursed is usually indicated by boxes of gloves, masks, etc. outside the patient's room, together with an appropriate notice affixed to the door. One of the greatest 'crimes' that one can commit is to ignore these signs and go straight into the room. The wrath of the ward sister may be exceeded only by that of the 'control of infection' sister or the bacteriologist!

If regular visits from a local church or chaplain are being made to a patient in hospital it may help to ask the nursing staff to record the fact on the Nursing Cardex. Some hospitals will have a special section of the Cardex where this sort of information can be recorded, together with details of whether or not a particular person should be contacted in the event of the patient being discharged or their condition deteriorating. Relationships will not be helped if clergy do not inform staff of their involvement and interest and later complain because they are not informed of the patient's death or discharge from hospital. However, no system is perfect, and even when staff are informed poor communication between staff can still lead to some information being lost!

Recognizing that staff also have needs can enhance the understanding of the role and usefulness of the chaplain/pastoral worker within the hospital. The support of staff and the involvement of the chaplain in various in-service training and support schemes for staff frequently arises out of the relationship that is built up with staff in the course of responses to quite specific religious requests. For example, late one night a chaplain is called to the maternity department where a baby who was live born, has subsequently died. The distressed mother has asked for her child to be baptized. There are various responses which a chaplain *might* make:

The chaplain may decline to go to the hospital that night on the grounds that there is little that can be done since the baby has already died and so he/she will visit in the morning.   OR

The chaplain might go to the unit, baptize the child and briefly see the mother before returning home.   OR

The chaplain might visit the unit and explain to the parent(s) that baptism is inappropriate but that they can have a service for the naming, blessing and commending of the child. After spending time with the parent(s) and conducting the appropriate service the chaplain may then seek an opportunity to talk with the staff about the situation, their feelings and expectations of each other and why baptism may not be appropriate in all cases. Depending on how busy the unit was at the time this might be shared over coffee in the team room, and give the staff a chance to care for the chaplain by listening to his/her feelings about the incident they have shared. It might also lead to an invitation for the chaplain to return on a later occasion and discuss the issues at one of the midwifery study seminars.

The Community

For most people who require help and advice at a time of sickness the first approach will be to a general practitioner, a pharmacist, dentist or optician. As appropriate these will either treat, advise or refer the person to a specialist or hospital service. These are not employed directly by the NHS but may contract their services to the NHS through a local Family Practitioner Committee.

From the point of view of pastoral care most of the people whom the pastor would visit at home will either have visited the GP at the surgery or have arranged for a home visit by the doctor. There is, therefore, a clearly identifiable person who has responsibility for the management of the sick person at home and for the treatment that is suitable for that person. In recent years there has been much discussion concerning the tension between autonomy and paternalism in medicine. Against the background of this debate a growing number of practices have patient participation groups which enable patients, doctors and other people relevant to the practice to meet together to decide how best to develop health care in that practice area. The local Community Health Council may also be involved, as may local clergy who work in the same area. In considering with whom one should liaise regarding healing services, the GP is the most obvious person in the community in order to avoid misunderstanding.

It is usually the GP who will make a referral to other health care workers in the community as appropriate to the particular patient. These would include the Community Nursing Service comprising community nurses, health visitors, community midwife, community psychiatric nurses, night sitters, geriatric visiting service or, if available, the services of a terminal care/support team. Other available services include chiropody and a variety of social services which the GP may apply for or ask for the involvement of the Area Social Worker (who is employed by the local authority not the health service). Some GPs have a social worker attached to their practice.

The various people who are involved in providing health care within the community will often be based at a health centre, clinic or general practice, but it does not necessarily mean that they will have easy access to colleagues of the same profession. In the larger geographical areas such people may not have much contact with colleagues from other professions either and, although some might enjoy working solo, others may find the isolation creates stress and vulnerability. This can be a difficulty where a single nurse is appointed to work with terminally ill people within a particular area. To work solely with dying people can be emotionally draining as well as physically demanding, and the absence of others to share this with can lead to great stress. Linking together the various health care workers is usually the task of the health authority's Unit Management Group (Community) but there may well be scope for initiative to be taken by the local church.

Co-operation between health care workers partly results from management structures but is far more dependent upon the quality of the inter-personal relationships that are established and the mutual trust and respect that grows with time. Clergy in the community will face similar problems to their colleagues in the hospital service, in that respect has to be earned and is not ours as of right. Wherever possible it can be a distinct advantage if clergy can establish and build relationships with the local GPs and others at the health centre, clinics or practice. It may be that the local church may be able to take the initiative in inviting those working within a particular area to meet together for lunch at the local church. This could of course be established on an ecumenical basis, as has happened in several parts of the country where doctor/clergy groups have been formed and then expanded to include other professionals. Sometimes this has remained as an informal group; elsewhere it has formed itself into a field group of the Institute of Religion and Medicine (see Appendix A). In addition to establishing links with the health workers in a particular locality many churches (as mentioned earlier in chapter 6) operate street warden schemes, with varying success, which seek to maintain contact with neighbours and to offer help and assistance as required. This has proved especially valuable for elderly, handicapped, or chronically sick people who do not need to go into hospital or long-term care if there is someone available to help them should the need arise.

Conclusion

No matter how much time one spends pastorally within the hospital, the attitudes of staff will be formed by the way we respond to pastoral calls. This is especially true in those instances where it becomes clear that the staff are seeking help and support as well as the patient and family. An understanding of the National Health Service and of the factors affecting morale and working relationships can help the pastor to respond more appropriately to evidence of staff stress and vulnerability.

Whilst staff in hospital and community rightly expect a prompt, reliable and professional response from those who share with them in the care of sick people, they nevertheless find it reassuring if we can also express *our* vulnerability and the fact that we don't have it all wrapped up and neatly packaged. So many of the pastoral situations which arise in hospital are not clear cut with easy and obvious answers. The ability of the chaplain to say, 'I don't know, I don't fully understand—but I believe that's all right,' can indeed be a saving grace in the midst of so much technological know-how, and on-going professional assessment, which may leave little space for the airing of doubts lest one looks foolish. Each chaplain or pastor will develop his or her own style and approach in relating to the institution and its structures. Whether one puts the emphasis regarding the chaplain's role on priest, prophet or clown (to quote one model, see Faber, 1971), it is the possibility of isolation and vulnerability that the chaplain has to come to terms with and which can be a most valuable asset and link with patients and staff, enabling him or her to be a key person in initiating and establishing ways of caring for the carers.

NINE

Ethical Considerations

---

*The doctor, traditionally a person of authority, now has his opinions
questioned by individuals and groups with increased medical
knowledge, with the result that the ethical implications of his
actions are under scrutiny as never before . . . Another change of
attitude with ethical implications concerns claims by non-medically
qualified people, that doctors should not have sole authority over
diagnosis, referral, treatment, the granting of access to resources,
and rehabilitation. This development has deep significance for
patients, for all the health professions, and for the health services.*
(BMA, *Handbook of Medical Ethics*, 1984, sections 5.1, 5.3)

The exploration of the values of health care is something
which can involve all who are concerned with the care of sick
people. Many of the sick people themselves also take an
active interest in the value judgements made by those who
care for their health. With the influence of the media many
members of the general public are now quite well informed
about medical matters, as well as many of the issues
surrounding the major ethical topics in medicine such as in
vitro fertilization, abortion, brain death, euthanasia and
research.

In response to this interest and concern, a large number of
books have appeared which discuss these big ethical issues,
and some suggestions for further reading on these topics
appear in Appendix C. From the point of view of pastoral
care, some chaplains will become very involved with these
topics and may be consulted by staff and patients in the
decision-making process, or they may serve on the 'ethical
practices committee' which monitors research within the local
health district. Whilst many pastors may not have a very
close involvement with such issues, they cannot fail to become
involved with some of the broad ethical aspects associated
with the provision of health care. For the most part ethics is

concerned with people and with issues of responsibility, duty and rights. These in turn involve consideration of confidentiality, autonomy and paternalism. This chapter focuses on some of these basic issues, since they are encountered more frequently than, and in many ways are basic to any consideration of, the more dramatic events.

Autonomy and Respect

To be an autonomous person is to have the ability to be able to choose for oneself or to be able to create and fulfil one's own plans and ambitions. Being a person is bound up with the ability to 'stand on one's own feet' or 'to know what one wants'. If someone has suffered an accident which has left them with a disability, friends may tend to help too much. They may feel that it is easier if they perform a task, 'to save you the trouble', rather than wait while the injured person tries to do it for themselves. Although the motive is to be helpful, it can have the effect of subtly eroding the nature of the person. We may applaud autonomy until another person's autonomy begins to create difficulties for us. However, to *respect* a person entails taking into account the fact that that person is self-determining, self-governing and has feelings, desires and reason. If we express this in terms of *rights* and *duties* then a patient's *rights* are the human rights of individuals: the freedom to choose; the rights to knowledge and dignity; and the right to self-determination. But a patient also has *duties*: to disclose all relevant information fully and frankly in order that a diagnosis can be made. The exchange between doctor/patient depends on this duty for, unless the truth is told, truth cannot be told in return. This has implications for the way in which we care for the person who happens to be ill and who may still wish to retain a measure of autonomy.

A focus for the consideration of autonomy and respect is the interaction which takes place between the sick person and a doctor, nurse, physiotherapist, or pastor, where decisions are made and there are several elements to this interaction.

Confidentiality

It is implicit that whatever is shared in a consultation or visit is confidential, and this is an important element in building a relationship of trust. Within the health service *any* information obtained in the course of pastoral work within a hospital is confidential — even the fact that a patient has been admitted. This fact has been extensively covered in the *Handbook on Hospital Chaplaincy* (1987, p. 39) and pastorally should not cause any great difficulty if the permission of patients is sought before any information is shared. However, most professionals work in multi-disciplinary teams and so the issue arises about how much information can be shared, and with whom. There are several levels of information which will be stored in many places, some more easily accessed than others, on the assumption that the patient has agreed to this sharing and that it remains confidential to the team. As an example, we may consider Jim and divide the information about him into four categories:

a. *Identification data.* Jim is a 34-year-old married man, living in an inner-city council flat. His wife attends the local church, but he doesn't. He has been admitted for removal of a gallstone.
b. *Medical.* Routine medical tests show a slightly enlarged heart. Examination of Jim's blood shows that he is HIV + and carries the AIDS virus. He is known to the sexually transmitted disease clinic.
c. *Social.* He has two children, both well, though one recently suspected of shop-lifting. He has only told this to the social worker. He is unemployed but his wife works in a corner shop.
d. *Psychological.* Anxious about operation and about child's possible thefts. He feels very anxious about finding a job. Recently he has suffered from impotence and this has caused stress in his marital relationship. He is very embarrassed about this and doesn't want anyone to know. Because of extra-marital relationships he has been treated in the sexually transmitted disease clinic and feels very guilty about this. Has asked for an AIDS test because of anxiety aroused by recent publicity.

Various questions arise about who should know what

about Jim. Does everybody need to know everything? How much should a pastoral visitor/chaplain want or *need* to know about Jim? How much can staff tell the local vicar who has been asked to visit by Jim's wife? How much should go on a health reference when Jim applies for a job? Who should know that Jim is HIV+? There are also issues of confidentiality relating to the storage of information concerning Jim which would need to be considered.

Communication

A feature of the meeting between the sick person and those who are caring which can preserve the autonomy and respect, is the way in which people take care over *courtesy*, *communication* and *listening*. Remembering names, introducing yourself, saying goodbye are all part of showing respect. Similarly, explaining treatment and symptoms to patients in ways they can understand without being patronized respects their intelligence and allows them a better chance of participating in the decision-making. This is not easy but is important to the development of trust and honesty in the relationship. Perhaps the most obvious aspect of trust and honesty is in relation to 'truth-telling'. Many of the sick people one meets pastorally are trying to come to terms with uncertainty. This uncertainty may be shared by the professional, since the doctor may not be 100 per cent sure how best to interpret a set of results and therefore what to tell the patient or family. The doctor will make various value judgements before deciding how to approach the patient. Patients and families may want answers to specific questions, but the professional may only be able to answer in terms of trends and probabilities. For example, if Jim asks the doctor, 'Will I die of AIDS?' he may not wish to be evasive yet may feel unable to give a straight 'Yes'/'No' answer. Telling the truth is a particular aspect of the problem of uncertainty in medical care.

In many situations the 'whole' truth is not told for what we might describe as 'very good reasons', such as that we don't know *all* the truth, the other person doesn't want to hear it, 'I don't think it is appropriate . . .', etc. Clearly in deciding what to tell Jim in answer to his question, 'Will I die of AIDS?', several factors need to be considered. What is the actual question that Jim is asking—is he only expecting a 'No' or is he preparing himself for a 'Yes' or a 'Maybe'. Listening to the patient can help us to be clearer about what the question is. Timing is important, since the implications of information don't always sink in at once. Telling the truth (as we know it) should include allowing the patient some choice in the management of the condition. Therefore, it can help to reflect on various aspects before entering into discussion with a sick person or family. Do we have the knowledge of the possible outcome of treatment and the prognosis to answer the questions the patient may ask? What attitudes have we regarding the sharing of information with patients? Are there times when we would *not* tell the truth, tell a lie, not tell the *whole* truth, or confront the person with the truth? It is tempting to assume that patients and families wish to know the truth, and that this will help them to cope, but this also assumes a great deal about how people might cope with the information.

Paternalism

Because of the different situations which we may face over 'telling the truth' it can be tempting to deal with it by restricting the person's autonomy and being very *paternalistic* in our approach. Paternalism is the protection of individuals from self-inflicted harm and decisions are taken, choices made, freedom inhibited, all for the good of the patient (as we see it). The words we use can sometimes betray a paternalistic approach: 'We're going to give you a test this morning'; 'If you're good we'll let you out at the weekend'; 'Now then, my dear, I'm going to give you communion'. The main problem with paternalism is that it makes decisions for others which they have a right to take for themselves: 'Just leave that to me' or 'You don't need to know all the details'. Some would argue that there is a place for paternalism. Thurston Brewin (1985) presents the argument for a degree of paternalism in medical consultations to avoid overloading patients with information that can become a burden. He maintains the need for a balance between informed consent and protection.

Can the patient be part of the team?

An important corollary of autonomy is a consideration of the contribution of the patient as part of the decision-making process. This is slightly different from 'truth-telling', in that the patient may not be given every item of medical information but his/her views and opinions may be sought and then represented at a team meeting. The amount of information given to a patient, or understood by a patient, may vary considerably and be an important factor to consider when obtaining consent for any procedure. For example, in connection with organ transplantation it is the practice in one unit for the transplant surgeon to convene a 'round table' discussion at which the various people involved with the care of the patient are present. This includes the chaplain who is often present to represent the patient and to reflect the wishes and feelings (concerning the proposed operation) of the patient and family. The patient will be seen by the various members of the team prior to the meeting and various tests and investigations performed. An effort is made to ensure that there is a good understanding by patient and family of the procedures and risks, so that any consent given is as informed as possible. In the course of the meeting the various items of information are collated and a decision made to include or not include the patient on the transplant list. A decision not to include the patient may be on surgical or medical grounds (unlikely to withstand an anaesthetic, or anatomically unsuitable) or on psychological grounds (patient poorly motivated to comply with pre- and post-operation requirements, unsupported by family, does not wish to consider operation, etc.) Where a patient is not thought a suitable candidate for transplantation a commitment is made by the team to provide on-going care and support for the patient and family lest the decision be seen as a rejection of the patient.

Being the patient's advocate and representing the wishes and feelings of the sick person may be a very important role for a pastor or hospital chaplain to undertake. Some patients find it very difficult to speak out at times and may *feel* under a certain amount of pressure to consent to an operation or a particular procedure or test. It can, therefore, be appropriate for a chaplain to meet with the ward staff or medical staff and discuss these issues on behalf of the patient. It may emerge that the patient has not properly understood the need or reason for the test or operation. The pressure that the patient is feeling may also not have been recognized. Similarly some families can feel under pressure to give consent to a post-mortem examination after a relative has died. Unless the coroner is involved they can refuse permission but may not feel strong enough to say so. Medical staff have no wish to act unethically in such matters, but they may not always be aware of the pressures felt by relatives when such requests are made. The pastor may be in a good position to fulfil a vital, though at times uncomfortable, role in ensuring that the patient's and family's rights are adequately protected.

Consent

Consent is a concept related to any relationship between patients and those providing health care. It may be defined as *granting to someone the permission to do something he would not have the right to do without such permission.* It is usual to find various adjectives attached to the word consent in clinical practice — 'implied', 'voluntary', 'informed', etc.

There are many reasons why consent should be obtained and is morally desirable. It maintains respect for individual autonomy and self-determination by the sick person through allowing them to say 'Yes' or 'No'. It also ensures that the patient is aware of the risks undertaken, although this is dependent upon the person who gives the information and the sick person's ability to comprehend what they are told. Because sick people are vulnerable there needs to be a way of protecting them from duress and of ensuring that the physician, or whoever, looks at his/her own motives for suggesting the operation or procedure. Having to explain and justify the treatment can also help the doctor or nurse in their own development as well as contributing to the wider debate of ethical issues among the general public. Some ethical committees, who monitor medical research, request that doctors who wish approval for ethical trials attach a statement in lay terms of the information that the doctor will give to the patient. This has a two-fold effect in that the committee can see what patients will be told and it ensures that the doctor also has to give careful thought on how to present the research protocol to the patient.

Clinical trials also raise ethical problems because, while it is necessary to make progress in understanding the nature, causation, prevention and treatment of disease, to do so may cause harm. This creates a dilemma between caring for the individual (the principle of non-maleficence or benevolence) and caring for the good of the majority (the utilitarian principle). This dilemma is most clearly seen when the health of the individual will not be promoted by the proposed treatment, although others might benefit in the future. The use of a control group or a placebo would be an example of this. A 'placebo' is a harmless pill or injection which allows assessment of the effect of 'giving something' to the patient to be compared with active treatment. In many cases the 'placebo effect' can be beneficial whereas the real drug may be of no benefit, or even harmful. The ethical problems involved are not always, therefore, straightforward.

The different adjectives indicate the various ways in which 'consent' is used in health care:

Implied consent suggests that consent can sometimes be taken for granted and that specific permission does not need to be obtained: confidentiality, certain treatments and examinations, being seen by medical students in a teaching hospital. There must be limits to what can be assumed.

Informed consent has been the subject of much discussion because of the difficulty of ensuring that the patient is adequately informed. Can a lay person ever be fully informed and how much information should a doctor reveal about possible rare side-effects? The question of competence also arises, since certain groups may not be able to comprehend the information given (e.g. children, unconscious patients, very distressed people and certain psychiatric patients). Since patients do not always fully understand, and therefore subsequently have doubts, they may wish to discuss it with the chaplain/pastor.

Voluntary consent implies that the patient consents of his own freewill and is not coerced or pressured to sign. However, some decisions may seem like a 'Hobson's choice', since a person with an inoperable tumour may not worry about distinctions between treatment, therapeutic research and non-therapeutic research but agree to anything on offer.

For consent to be valid, therefore, there needs to be both a disclosure and a comprehension of information. The consent obtained then needs to be given voluntarily and the patient should be competent to give that consent. However, attention also needs to be given to questions such as: How much information? Is it really understood? Can the consent ever be fully voluntary? Sometimes a patient will refuse to give consent for a treatment that the physician knows would be beneficial, thus creating a tension between respect for the autonomy of the patient and the desire of the physician (governed by the principle of benevolence) to help the patient.

Quality of Life

Quality of life is another fundamental concept which is reflected in so many aspects of health care though it is not so easy to define. There seems to be no universally accepted definition, though most would agree that quality of life relates to the individual person and that it is best perceived by that person, that it changes with time, and that it must be related to all aspects of life. One way of assessing it is to look at the individual's hopes and aspirations in relation to that individual's actual present state. The term 'quality of life' is often linked with 'quantity of life', and the hope in medicine is that whilst seeking to improve the patient's quality of life it may also prolong survival. This may perhaps be twinned with the principle that doctors should not only 'do no harm' but should also endeavour to 'do good' by increasing the benefit to others.

Where there is a trade-off between quality and quantity it cannot be assumed that patients will always choose quality. Thus in a study of patients with cancer of the larynx (McNeil *et al.*, 1981) quantity was the first choice. Where there is a local cancer not extending beyond the larynx, but advanced enough to cause complete immobility of the vocal chords resulting in hoarseness of voice, a laryngectomy leads to a three-year survival rate of 60 per cent, but with permanent loss of speech. Alternatively, radiation therapy offers a reduced survival (30—40 per cent to three years) but retains normal or near normal speech. Given this information 81 per cent said they would opt for surgery (with a greater survival rate) even though it would result in irreversible loss of voice.

Issues relating to quality/quantity feature strongly in

connection with the care of the newborn and in terminal care (at all ages). The decisions which may need to be made relating to the prolongation of life by the use of technology raise many issues in this area, as well as whether life should be preserved at all costs. There may also be conflict between the needs and wishes of the patient and those of the family, and the pastor may be drawn in to 'arbitrate'. Another aspect is the economic one since, with limited resources, treatment which is palliative (and only improves quality) may be given a lower priority in funding than high-tech potentially curative treatments. Various measures and indices have been suggested to assist in deciding on priorities of health care. These often include factors relating to quality of life such as work, recreation, physical and mental suffering, communication, sleep, dependence on others, feeding, bowel and bladder function and sexual activity. The scoring may be undertaken by staff, or patient/family, or both.

Making decisions about rationing resources can be painful, and health economists have tried to ease this by introducing the concept of quality adjusted life years (QALY) which is a measurement of health based on longevity and quality of life:

> The essence of a QALY is that it takes a year of healthy life expectancy to be worth 1, but regards a year of unhealthy life expectancy as worth less than 1. Its precise value is lower the worse the quality of life of the unhealthy person (which is what the quality adjusted bit is all about). If being dead is worth zero, it is, in principle, possible for QALY to be negative, i.e., for the quality of someone's life to be judged worse than being dead.
>
> The general idea is that a beneficial health care activity is one that generates a positive amount of QALYs, and that an efficient health care activity is one where the cost per QALY is as low as it can be. A high priority health care activity is one where the cost-per-QALY is low, and a low priority activity is one where cost-per-QALY is high. (Williams, 1985)

The acceptance of the use of QALYs rests on the belief that, given the choice, any person would prefer a shorter, healthier life to one with a longer survival but having severe disability. However, as shown above, there are many people who will make a trade-off by accepting a decrease in quality of life in order to prolong their survival. It is also important not to confuse a low quality of life with meaninglessness or being of little worth, since there may still be potential for meaning and growth, even in the face of gross disability. Whilst QALYs might be of value in the large-scale planning of health care and the distribution of budgets, they may not ease the problems for the doctor facing an individual patient in need. The allocation of limited resources is a major ethical issue at present, focusing, as it does, on issues relating to quality of life and on the way in which decisions are made.

Conclusion

Those involved in caring pastorally for the sick may, from time to time, find that they are invited to join with patients, families or health-care staff in examining the various ethical issues that arise in health care. This is a multi-disciplinary undertaking and relates very closely to the quality of the care that is given and not just to technical excellence, important though that is. Whilst we may not necessarily, therefore, be involved in the more dramatic ethical issues in medicine, the very nature of the pastoral relationship has an ethical aspect which should not be ignored since, 'Only intense personalized involvement can create the moral environment in which care is not only excellent but also a true response to human need' (Levine, 1977).

TEN

Supporting Those Who Care

———

God grant me the serenity
To accept the things I cannot change,
The courage to change the things I can,
And the wisdom to know the difference.
(Reinhold Niebuhr)

When seeking to understand an experience, such as illness, it can help if we can acquire appropriate knowledge as well as have the support and companionship of others while we undertake that search. Niebuhr's prayer points us to one source of that knowledge, or wisdom, namely God. It also emphasizes the importance of developing our relationship with him through attending to our spiritual life. But we are not alone in this search for meaning, since caring for sick people will raise questions concerning ultimate issues and the purpose of life for other carers as well. It has been suggested earlier that this search for meaning is a spiritual search (chapter 3) and at times this can make people feel vulnerable and uncomfortable, since it can create uncertainties about faith and belief. If we are isolated spiritually we are especially vulnerable and may develop a defensive, protective attitude towards our own beliefs which can affect the degree to which we can be open to those we care for, lest they perceive our spiritual shallowness.

Genuineness in pastoral care is crucial and costly, and rightly so, for we need to give something of ourselves in most of our encounters with those who are sick. If we are to be able to 'be there', and to enter into the suffering and uncertainty of the other person, we need to feel supported and reasonably sure of our foundation. However, spirituality is not simply a preparation or technique for doing pastoral care better. It is more a matter of our inner spiritual life being the means by which we can avail ourselves of the wisdom of God and root our pastoral care in the context of his love and support, acknowledging our dependence upon him and not just on our own counselling skills.

The support which the pastor needs as an individual is also relevant to others who are involved in the care of sick people, whether staff member, pastoral visitor or relative. This support may be offered in various ways:

1. Informally by listening, offering appropriate reassurance, and perhaps interpreting the patient's behaviour. A touch of the arm, a drink in the pub, a few words of appreciation, a bunch of flowers, are informal ways of caring for each other which should not be under-rated in importance.

2. Through a semi-formal statement of gratitude or valuing of the other person perhaps at a social gathering. There may also be a semi-formal group meeting to discuss general problems with the opportunity to share thoughts and feelings.

3. A more formal group or individual sharing activity facilitated by someone *outside* of the group who are undertaking the care. Such a group would usually have clearly defined boundaries and task.

What is central to all these approaches is the need to value each other as *people* and for the people concerned to feel that their feelings and contribution to the work are valued. This can make us more able to recognize a personal inadequacy to cope in certain situations and to be clearer about our own strengths and weaknesses. In this way we can be affirmed as a person and enabled to grow in understanding and confidence by being realistic about what we *can* offer by way of support and care to others in need in contrast to what we would *like* to offer to them. An important part of this is being able to acknowledge that, whilst caring for the sick can be satisfying, at times it is deeply distressing and we make a terrible mess of it. For this sharing to happen there needs to be a space or opportunity which feels sufficiently safe and accepting to allow the expression of feelings and reactions relating to the people and events involved.

Support for Relatives and Pastoral Visitors

The family of someone who is ill can often suffer as much if not more than the patient, especially where the sick person is a child. Failure to offer sufficient and appropriate support can result in the relative becoming as much a 'patient' as the sick person. A frequent source of worry is lack of information and the uncertainty which that creates. It can be very helpful and supportive if nurses and doctors can give adequate, truthful information and regular up-dates on the patient's condition, preferably without being asked. Consulting with relatives (and also when possible with the patient) can enable them to be more relaxed and co-operative over the care of the patient.

Many of the fears experienced by families may be quite groundless and easily dispersed by facts. However, relatives can sometimes feel that they are being foolish and therefore be quite hesitant to bother 'the busy staff' with their 'silly worries'. Making an opportunity for relatives to share what *they* feel is important and implies that we should actively listen to them and show that we value the feelings and reactions they express. Such an opportunity may need to be repeated since the ability to hear and register information is greatly impaired when people are worried and anxious. It may be that the *patient*'s behaviour and reactions are causing distress to the family and some interpretation may help them understand and feel able to continue caring.

For example: a wife was very distressed after visiting her husband. He was in hospital for investigation of a suspected growth and he had just spent the past hour picking a fight with his wife until she was reduced to tears, whereupon he told her she was too feeble to be of any use to him and had better go home. She was convincing herself that their marriage was ending and it took quite a time (and many tissues) before she was able to acknowledge that he was frightened of losing her, felt very vulnerable and was hitting out at her as the only safe person to hit! Whilst this experience was still acutely painful, listening to her hurt and interpreting some of the behaviour did help her to continue caring and visiting. In some situations there may be underlying feelings of resentment or guilt about the restrictions imposed on the relative by caring for the sick person. It might also emerge that the relationship has always been difficult and now has become impossible, in which case it can be very difficult to leave someone who is needy. Having someone to share such feelings with may enable the relative to stay, or find the strength to leave.

Interpreting treatment and routine can help relatives and others to feel less frightened and inadequate in specialist areas such as on the intensive therapy unit or when a patient is being barrier nursed. Encouraging the relative to make physical contact, to talk to the patient, to assist in washing or generally caring for the sick person can all help to ease fear and inadequacy, as mentioned earlier (chapter 5).

It is very easy to take relatives and pastoral visitors for granted and to assume that because they have cared in the past they will continue to care in the future. However, many relatives can become exhausted and value a break from the visiting or the caring. If the person is being cared for at home this may be provided by the sick person being taken into hospital for respite care, by the provision of a night-sitter, or by someone else taking over the home care whilst the relative goes away for a holiday. It may be that the local church can undertake this sort of short-term care to enable families to cope with the longer-term problem of care. Within the hospital one often sees relatives spending long hours in the intensive therapy unit dayroom, or keeping long vigils by the bedside. Whilst their need to be there is easily understood, nevertheless they must also look after themselves so that they can be in a reasonable frame of mind and body when, and if, the patient recovers. They may, therefore, require gentle encouragement (not bullying) to eat, rest, and go outside for fresh air every so often.

There is an inter-relatedness to caring for sick people which means that it is not really possible to separate out care/support for one group without also referring to the needs of other groups. Each group concerned with the sick person may offer a measure of support towards each other, but they may also compete with one another in respect of their own needs. Figure 1 illustrates one way in which the three major groups offering care to the sick person may inter-relate with each other and the possibilities that exist for mutual support and care—not least to and from the patient who may, if permitted to do so, give much to those who come to be there and to share in whatever capacity.

1. *The interface between the family and the health care professionals* reflects the situations where the family undertake a share in the caring/nursing of the sick person. The family may be taught how to perform various tasks by the nursing staff and to recognize their own limits. The fact that the family is assisting in this way can relieve some of the pressure on the health care staff and thus be supportive to them. Many families also give much to staff by their example, fortitude and friendliness.

2. *The interface between the family and those offering pastoral care* may be evidenced in various ways. Those involved pastorally may enable the family to discover meaning in the experience of illness in addition to, perhaps, being able to offer practical help through the involvement of the local church (perhaps by offering transport to the hospital). The

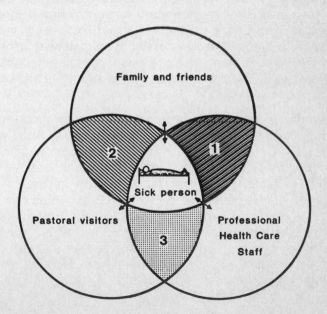

Figure 1: The inter-relatedness of caring

family may reciprocate by providing 'cups of tea' for the visitor, or through the sharing together in acts of worship which might be as healing for the visitor as the visited. Sometimes the family will show appreciation and care for the pastor by not calling him/her out in the middle of the night on occasions when they feel they can keep going until the morning. Alternatively, the pastoral visitor may sit with the patient at night in order that the relatives may have some sleep.

3. *The interface between the health care professionals and those offering pastoral care* may represent the occasions when the pastor may undertake an aspect of the professional's role (e.g. chasing up requests for handrails in the bathroom, or a commode, which seem to be a long time arriving). At times the health care staff may join in the pastoral role by themselves offering an overt ministry to the patient or sharing in that of the pastor in a more open way.

4. *The sick person* is central to all this and, whilst in many ways the recipient of all the care, may also contribute a great deal to all involved. The greatest teacher of pastoral care and professional health care can be the patient if only we can *listen to* and *be with* the sick person in an open way. Not only is this of benefit to us but it also goes a long way to maintaining, or perhaps restoring, the dignity of the person who is ill.

The overlap of the different roles of the people concerned can be very supportive and can mitigate against isolation in caring. It can also lead to fuzziness and uncertainty about why one is there and what one expects to achieve; this reminds us again of the importance of focus in pastoral care (chapter 5). The element of competitiveness which can arise when overlap occurs can cause defensive behaviour and stress because others are performing tasks which we feel are more properly ours—and perhaps we perceive that they are doing them better than we might! Apart from making us feel redundant they can create deep feelings of rivalry and jealousy which then detract from the care we give to the patient. This factor becomes even more important when considering the problems created by multi-disciplinary teams and support groups as discussed later in this chapter.

In some units, because the patients all have a similar medical condition, the staff and relatives may arrange meetings for families and staff. These meetings may be of a social nature, or also for fund raising. They provide a very useful forum for the exchange of information about the particular illness, for sharing ways of coping, and to provide support for each other. The groups may be composed of the families of people with renal failure, haemophilia, leukaemia, asthma, heart disease, strokes, or rheumatism, etc. Self-help groups and family groups can be supportive to family, patient and staff, provided there is sufficient professional help available to ensure that the facts shared are accurate and that people are not being misinformed.

Support Groups

One way of providing an opportunity for sharing has been through the creation of 'support groups' which have been based in the community, within a hospital ward or within a hospice or health centre. Some of these groups are composed of members of one profession only, whilst others are multi-disciplinary. Some use a facilitator from outside the group and others nominate one of the group or unit staff to act as facilitator. Within the Church of England diocese of London a system of support groups was set up in 1977 which, although intended primarily for the clergy and those who work with them pastorally, has resulted in the formation of some very interesting multi-disciplinary groups. These are locally based and co-led by a male/female pair who have received training and been accredited for the work. There are usually eight people in the group, plus the two leaders, and they meet weekly or fortnightly. The objectives of the group are to enable members to explore issues arising from their work and the way in which these were handled. Members may be helped to see themselves in a new light and to widen their understanding. Over the time that they work together the mutual trust within the group may permit more personal matters to be shared and examined. Thompson states: 'These schemes are in an early stage of development and are small in comparison with the needs which they could be meeting if they were able to expand. The "take-up" rate among clergy is low, and leaders face disappointments as they set about recruitment' (Thompson and Thompson, 1987, p. 274). This would seem to indicate the need for diversity in the forms in which support is made available to clergy and others, since not everyone will feel able to work within a group setting and may resist *formal* support in any form.

In considering support within the context of health care it can be helpful to consider the provision and receipt of health care within an organization such as a hospital, in terms of the inter-relationships that exist within the institution and between the institution and the outside world. One theoretical framework which allows us to gain some understanding of the processes which take place in these interactions is that known as 'General Systems Theory'. Although general systems theory originated in physics and thermodynamics (in the 1940s), it can be applied to a living system. If we do this we can show that what we otherwise take as a static state is in fact in a state of dynamic equilibrium with continual change. An individual or an organization may be viewed as an *open* system concerned with the management of the boundary between the individual/group and the outside world in order that the work within the system can be carried out. (By using the word 'open' it is implied that the system can respond to stimuli and to change.)

When open systems theory is applied to an organization or a working group it highlights the managerial role. The organization is then seen as a living system, open to and in contact with its environment, where boundaries are very important to the organization being able to achieve a dynamic equilibrium with that environment. The system has to constantly monitor and react to the pressures of the world outside, and failure to do so will increase anxiety, internal fighting and avoidance of the real issues.

However, the work of continually monitoring and reacting with the environment, and maintaining an appropriate internal organization, is an energy-consuming task that can create intense anxieties. If, for instance, an old-established family firm realises that its product and methods are no longer appropriate to the 1970's, the anxiety may be so strong that energy is withdrawn from managing the boundary and used in a whole variety of defence mechanisms to avoid the real issue. For a time these will protect the firm from the need to change and adapt, but unless it eventually faces up to this harsh reality, it will eventually go bankrupt. (DeBoard, 1978)

Setting up a working group to provide support for staff

An interesting account of the setting up of a support group for nursing staff (by a ward sister and a hospital chaplain) was published in the magazine *Hospital Chaplain* (Martin and Dowd, 1985). Their 'Monday Afternoon Group' represents one example of a working group and the wide variety of topics they shared over a six-week period. There are many different ways of establishing and running a support group, but the following suggestions cover items to be borne in mind at an early stage. If the group is to have a chance of succeeding, there will need to be careful preparation and negotiation with relevant people in the organization—management and workers:

a. *Who will the group members be?* Will it be the total staff group, single or multi-disciplinary, only those at a particular level of responsibility, or only representative people (and if so selected by whom)?

b. *How will the group be brought together*, and who will tell them what and when about the reason and purpose of the group?

c. *Boundaries of the group.* When and where to meet; how often (weekly, fortnightly?); for how long $(1-1\frac{1}{2}$ hours). Confidentiality is a key issue and can be very relevant when discussing the group's relationship with management and 'reporting back'. Confidentiality also closely relates to building up trust within the group. People will not feel free to share difficult or painful issues in a group with 'leaky boundaries' and where people may gossip about the group in other settings.

d. *What task will the group be engaged in?* What things can be brought to the group? What do those in authority want, what do the members want, what does the leader/consultant/facilitator want? By definition a 'working group' has work as its primary focus, i.e. the care of sick people. The main task, therefore, must be work-related and not personal/family problems or therapy. It may be that in the course of the group it emerges that an individual's personal life problems are affecting that person's performance at work. It would not be the task of the group to try to 'solve' this person's problems but to identify what was happening and assist him/her, perhaps, in obtaining help elsewhere. The task may seem somewhat vague at first, but might be expressed as 'sharing together concerns which arise in the course of our work, in order to do the job more effectively'. The way of working may vary from a 'case-centred' approach to the absence of any agenda, with people being free to bring any current issue to a group meeting.

e. *What is the consultant/facilitator's role to be?* In contrast to a supervisor, it should be enabling but not taking responsibility for the work. The ownership of the problems remains with the group and is not off-loaded on to the consultant. In respect of responsibility the facilitator looks after the boundaries, or ensures that someone else does, and helps to keep the group to the agreed task.

Each working group will explore issues arising out of the nature of the work and the people involved in the group. A selection of topics which might be explored by a group is included to illustrate something of the scope and range.

1. *Expectations of myself and of each other*

Many of the problems which are experienced in work groups relate to the various expectations that people have of each other, but which may never actually be expressed. If these cannot be identified and talked about people may find themselves falling short on performance and receiving negative feedback. This can feel quite unfair when one has not been informed what is the required standard. Some expectations will be unrealistic or idealistic on either a personal or a corporate level and between them can cause tension and anxiety. This is represented diagrammatically in Figure 2.

If these anxieties cannot be resolved a sense of failure will develop which can lead to our undertaking unrealistic workloads as we strive to fulfil an unclear expectation. The result can be exhaustion, lack of job satisfaction, and increased

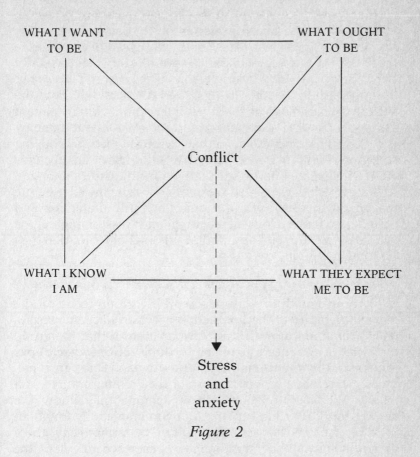

Figure 2

staff turnover and sickness rate. A facilitator may be able to help the work group establish how far this situation is the result of the individual concerned, the work group itself, or the management structure.

2. *Extent to which people and their feelings are valued*

It can be very supportive if you find that your feelings are valued by other people and that you are listened to and given permission and the space you need to share what you feel about a particular situation. If such an opportunity is not made available then people may feel 'dumped' with certain feelings because no one is prepared to listen. It is not only in terminal care that people may be left carrying powerful feelings which have been projected on to them by others; for example, a patient who was totally paralysed and unable to speak had the effect of making several staff members feel quite disabled and incompetent. These staff were not incompetent in other settings, and through sharing the situation it became clear that their interaction with the patient was a key factor. The patient would scream without stopping until a staff member did something wrong — such as dropping something — and then the patient would giggle. The feelings which this created in the staff ranged from distress to anger, feelings which they needed to express and acknowledge before they could free themselves of this powerful interaction and consider suitable ways of eliciting and responding to the patient's needs, or else accept that this was one situation they could not get right.

3. *Tensions arising from different disciplines working together*

Many problems dealt with in a working group focus on the tensions relating to the interaction between different disciplines. Communication is one obvious area in that the group may frequently need to clarify what various disciplines understand by the terms they normally use. This can sometimes mean that a group member or the facilitator may ask a 'naive' question to which others assume they know the answer, until asked to explain. Many misunderstandings can be cleared up in this way. In addition to terminology, there may be a lack of understanding about each other's role in the team and where the boundaries lie. This frequently leads back to an examination of expectations and assumptions and can uncover ways in which people may have been stereotyped. 'Oh well, all doctors/social workers/clergy think like that.' It is possible, by focusing on the *process* going on between the people in the group rather than the *content* being expressed, to see the inter-relationships within the organization reflected or mirrored with the group. Sometimes the 'problem' presented in the group is a wider problem of the institution which the institution is ignoring. This can leave a group feeling that they are a 'dumping ground' and impotent to effect change.

By focusing on 'who owns the problem?', or which aspects of the situation are mine and which belong to others, the group can be enabled to challenge the organization and themselves initiate change. There are, however, strong defence mechanisms within organizations which can make this difficult to achieve.

4. *Recognition of some of the defensive ways in which people try to cope with anxiety, tension and change*

Resistance to change within an organization, together with personal ineffectiveness, are often caused by defensive techniques developed by individuals in order to combat high anxiety levels and maintain equilibrium. This process was studied by Menzies who looked at the nursing service in a large London teaching hospital in 1970. Among several findings she noted that decision-making can become a life and death matter in hospital and generates much anxiety. The defence against this anxiety is what Menzies called 'ritual task performance'. Each nurse was taught to work by following an extremely rigid task-list, and the attitude inculcated was that *every* task is a matter of life and death, to be treated with appropriate seriousness. Consequently, student nurses were actively discouraged from using their discretion and initiative.

> The needs of the members of the organisation to use it in the struggle against anxiety leads to the development of socially structured defence mechanisms which appear as elements in the structure, culture and mode of functioning of the organisation. A social defence system develops over time as the result of collusive interaction and agreement, often unconscious, between members of the organisation as to what form it will take. The socially structured defence mechanisms then tend to become an aspect of external reality with which old and new members of the institution must come to terms. (Menzies, 1970, p. 10)

Change in such situations will be resisted, since it entails a restructuring of the social defences, with the consequence that anxiety becomes more open and intense. As a result the foci of power and influence are shifted, requiring that others participate in the process of change lest the change should lead to suspicion, anger and rejection. However, systems *can* change, as has been illustrated in recent years by the way in which the nursing profession has moved away from task-centred nursing to the problem-solving/person-centred approach of the 'nursing process' which invites the nurse to become involved with the patient as a person from the earliest stage of hospitalization.

Conclusion

Within this chapter we have looked at various ways in which those who care for sick people may obtain the support they require to continue with that caring. This book has also focused upon *pastoral* care in particular; and the essence of pastoral care is that it deals with ultimate issues (see p. 65). In order to enable people to face these issues we may need to acquire and develop skills in counselling or inter-personal relationships. However, we must not overlook the fact that all of this takes place within the context of *our* relationship with God, since our sufficiency to fulfil this task is not of ourselves — it is of God (2 Cor. 3.5).

APPENDIX A:

Addresses

Church Organizations

Churches' Council for Health and Healing (CCHH), St Marylebone Parish Church, Marylebone Road, London, NW1 5LT.

Guild of Health, Edward Wilson House, 26 Queen Anne Street, London W1M 9LB.

Guild of St Raphael, St Marylebone Parish Church, Marylebone Road, London NW1 5LT.

Hospital Chaplaincies Council (HCC), Church House, Great Smith Street, Westminster, London SW1P 3NZ.

Hospital Chaplaincy Board, Free Church Federal Council, 27 Tavistock Square, London WC1H 9HH.

Hospital Chaplains' Fellowship (HCF), c/o Chaplain's Office, The Royal Free Hospital, Pond Street, Hampstead, London NW3 2QG.

Institute of Religion and Medicine (IRM), St Marylebone Parish Church, Marylebone Road, London NW1 5LT.

National Association of Whole-Time Hospital Chaplains (NAWTHC), c/o Chaplain's Office, Royal United Hospital, Combe Park, Bath, Avon BA1 3NG.

Support Organizations

The Compassionate Friends, 6 Denmark Street, Bristol BS1 5DQ.

Cruse, Cruse House, 126 Sheen Road, Richmond, Surrey TW9 1UR.

153

The Foundation for the Study of Infant Deaths, 15 Belgrave Square, London SW1 8PS.

The Miscarriage Association, 18 Stoneybrook Close, West Bretton, Wakefield, West Yorkshire WF4 4TP.

The Stillbirth and Neonatal Death Society (SANDS), Argyle House, 29—31 Euston Road, London NW1 2SD.

Some Suggested Topics for a Training Programme

These are based on the HCC handbook *'I was Sick . . .'* — A *Guide for Introducing Chaplaincy Visitors to Work in Hospital.*

1   An overview of the hospital.
2   The work of the doctor.
3   The work of the nurse.
4   The ward routine (courtesy, etiquette, patient's viewpoint).
5   Chaplaincy/staff relationships.
6   Visiting the patient: forming a relationship.
7   Basic visiting/communication skills.
8   The chaplain's *expectations* of himself.
9   Chaplaincy visitors' own *expectations*: of themselves, the chaplain, patients and staff.
10   God's love in hospital. Prayer in the midst of pain. Spiritual/religious needs and responses.
11 and 12 Special areas of work within the hospital — with special reference to areas where visitors will work.

APPENDIX C:

Select Bibliography on Ethical Issues in Health Care

Autton, N., *Doctors Talking*. Mowbray, Oxford, 1984.

Boyd, K. M., Melia, K. M. and Thompson, I. E., *Nursing Ethics*. Churchill Livingstone, Edinburgh, 1983.

Campbell, A. V., *Moral Dilemmas in Medicine* (3rd edn). Churchill Livingstone, Edinburgh, 1984.

Downie, R. S. and Calman, K. C., *Healthy Respect—Ethics in Health Care*. Faber, London, 1987.

Duncan, A. S., Dunstan, G. R. and Welbourn, R. B., *Dictionary of Medical Ethics* (2nd edn). Darton, Longman and Todd, London, 1981.

Glover, Jonathan, *Causing Death and Saving Lives*. Penguin, Harmondsworth, 1977.

Illich, I., *Limits to Medicine (Medical Nemesis)*. Penguin, Harmondsworth, 1978.

Kennedy, I., *The Unmasking of Medicine*. Paladin, London, 1983.

Ladd, J., *Ethical Issues Relating to Life and Death*. OUP, New York, 1979.

Phillips, M. and Dawson, J., *Doctor's Dilemmas*. Harvester, Brighton, 1985.

Warnock, M., *A Question of Life*. Basil Blackwell, Oxford, 1985.

Weir, R. F., *Ethical Issues in Death and Dying* (2nd edn). Columbia, New York, 1986.

In addition, the *Journal of Medical Ethics* is a valuable source of comment on many of the ethical issues in health care.

References

Ainsworth-Smith, I. and Speck, P. (1982), *Letting Go: Caring for the Dying and Bereaved*. SPCK, London.

Archbishop of Canterbury's Commission (1958), *The Church's Ministry of Healing*. Church Information Office, London.

Archbishop of Canterbury's Commission (1985), *Faith in the City*. Church Information Office, London.

Asher, R. (1972), 'Malingering', in *Health and Disease — a Reader*, ed. N. Black, D. Boswell *et. al.* Open University Press, Milton Keynes.

Autton, N. (1986), *Pain — An Exploration*. Darton, Longman and Todd, London.

Bailey, P. (1967), *At the Jerusalem*. Jonathan Cape, London.

Blows, D. (1987), 'Structure' in *A Dictionary of Pastoral Care*, ed. A. Campbell. SPCK, London.

Board of Social Responsibility (1986), *AIDS — Some Guidelines for Pastoral Care*. Church House Publishing, London.

Brewin, T. (1985), 'Truth, Trust and Paternalism', *The Lancet*, 31 Aug. 1985, pp. 490 — 2.

British Medical Association (1984), *The Handbook of Medical Ethics*. BMA, London.

Browning, J. W. (1986), *Chaplaincy Modes in Mental Health*. Trent Regional Health Authority, Sheffield.

Burton, L. (1975), *The Family Life of Sick Children*. Routledge and Kegan Paul, London.

Campbell, A. (1981), *Moderated Love — A Theology of Professional Care*. SPCK, London.

Carr, W. (1985), *Brief Encounters — Pastoral Care through the Occasional Offices*. SPCK, London.

Causley, C. (1983), *Collected Poems — 1951 — 1975*. Macmillan, London.

Chrisman, N. (1977), 'The Health Seeking Process: An Approach to the Natural History of Illness', *Culture,*

Medicine and Psychiatry, 1 (4), pp. 351—77.

Churches' Council for Health and Healing (1986), *Guidelines for Those Involved in Healing Ministry,* Occasional Papers, no. 3. St Marylebone Parish Church, London.

Clebsch, W. A. and Jaekle, C. R. (1967), *Pastoral Care in Historical Perspective*, Harper, New York.

Cronin, A. J. (1983 edn), *The Citadel.* New England Library, Sevenoaks.

DeBoard, R. (1978), *The Psychoanalysis of Organisations.* Tavistock, London.

Department of Health and Social Security (1976), *RAWP: Report of the Resource Allocation Working Party*, DHSS, London.

Department of Health and Social Security (1986), 'Appointment of Hospital Chaplains', *PM (86) Section 4*, DHSS, London.

Dyne, G. (1981), *Bereavement Visiting.* King Edward's Hospital Fund for London, London.

Eadie, H. (1973), 'Stress and the Clergyman—Health of Scottish Clergymen' part 2, *Contact* 42, pp. 22—35.

Eadie, H. (1975), 'The Helping Personality', *Contact* 49, pp. 2—17.

Eadie, H. (1987), 'Pastor: Personality', in *A Dictionary of Pastoral Care*, ed. A. Campbell. SPCK, London.

Egan, G. (1982), *The Skilled Helper* (2nd edn). Brooks/Cole, Belmont, USA.

Engel, G. I. (1977), 'The Need for a New Medical Model: A Challenge for Biomedicine', *Science* 196 (4286), pp. 129—36.

Faber, H. (1971), *Pastoral Care in the Modern Hospital.* SCM Press, London.

Foskett, J. (1984), *Meaning in Madness: The Pastor and the Mentally Ill.* SPCK, London.

Foskett, J. (1987), 'Pastor: Personal and Family Life,' in *A Dictionary of Pastoral Care*, ed. A. Campbell. SPCK, London.

Frankl, V. E. (1987 edn), *Man's Search for Meaning.* Hodder and Stoughton, London.

Grainger, R. (1979), *Watching for Wings: Theology and Mental Illness in a Pastoral Setting.* Darton, Longman and Todd, London.

Grainger, R. (1984), *A Place Like This—A Guide to Life in a Psychiatric Hospital*. Churchman, Worthing.

Hamel-Cooke, C. (1986), *Health is for God*. Arthur James, London.

Harwood, A. (1971), 'The Hot-Cold Theory of Disease: Implications for Treatment of Puerto Rican Patients', *Journal of the American Medical Association*, 216, pp. 1153—68.

Henley, A. (1979), *Asian Patients in Hospital and at Home*. King Edward's Hospital Fund for London.

Hospital Chaplaincies Council (1986), *'I was Sick . . .'—A Guide for Introducing Chaplaincy Visitors to Work in Hospital*. Hospital Chaplaincies Council, London.

Hospital Chaplaincies Council (1987), *A Handbook on Hospital Chaplaincy*. HCC, London.

Jacobs, M. (1976), 'Naming and Labelling', *Contact*, 54, pp. 3, 8.

Jacobs, M. (1985), *Swift to Hear: Facilitating Skills in Listening and Responding*. SPCK, London.

Jacobs, M. (1986), *The Presenting Past—An Introduction to Practical Psycho-Dynamic Counselling*. Harper and Row, London.

Kitzinger, S. (1977), *Education and Counselling for Childbirth*. Bailliere-Tindall, London.

Kübler-Ross, E. (1970), *On Death and Dying*. Tavistock, London.

Lambourne, R. A. (1963), *Community, Church and Healing*. Darton, Longman and Todd, London.

Levine, M. (1977), 'Ethics: Nursing Ethics and the Ethical Nurse', *American Journal of Nursing*, 77 (5), pp. 845—9.

MacDonald, B. (1962), *The Plague and I*. Penguin, Harmondsworth.

McNeil, B. J., Weichselbaum, R. and Pauker, S. G. (1981), 'Speech and Survival: Trade-offs between Quality and Quantity of Life in Laryngeal Cancer', *New England Journal of Medicine*, 305, pp. 982—7.

Marinker, M. (1975), 'Why Make People Patients?', *Journal of Medical Ethics*, 1.2, p. 82.

Martin, T. and Dowd, O. (1985), 'The Monday Afternoon Group: An Attempt to Facilitate a Nursing Staff Support Group', *Hospital Chaplain*, Hospital Chaplains' Fellowship.

Menzies, I. E. P. (1970), *The Functioning of Social Systems as a Defence against Anxiety.* Tavistock Institute of Human Relations, London.

Our Ministry and Other Faiths—a Booklet for Hospital Chaplains (1983). CIO, London.

Parsons, T. (1951), *The Social System.* Free Press, New York.

Potter, D. (1986), *The Singing Detective.* Faber, London.

Quoist, M. (1965), 'The Hospital', *Prayers of Life*, Gill and Macmillan, Dublin.

Raggett, G. (1986), 'Music with the Elderly', *Hospital Chaplain*, Hospital Chaplains' Fellowship.

Ramsay, I. (1969), 'The Theology of Salvation' in E. Claxton and H. A. C. McKay (eds.), *Medicine, Morals and Man.* Blandford, London.

Royal College of Obstetricians and Gynaecologists (1985), *Report of the RCOG Working Party on the Management of Perinatal Deaths.* RCOG, 27 Sussex Place, London NW1.

Saltzberger-Wittenberg, I. (1986), *Psycho-Analytic Insight and Relationships.* Routledge and Kegan Paul, London.

Scambler, A., Scambler, G. and Craig, D. (1981), 'Kinship and Friendship Networks and Women's Demand for Primary Care', *Journal of the Royal College of General Practitioners* 26, pp. 746—50.

Smith, JoAnn K. (1977), *Free Fall.* SPCK, London.

Speck, P. W. (1970), 'Visiting in a Female Psycho-Geriatric Ward', *British Journal of Psychiatry*, vol. 117, pp. 93—4.

Speck, P. W. (1978), *Loss and Grief in Medicine.* Bailliere Tindall, London.

Sullivan, H. S. (1955), *The Interpersonal Theory of Psychiatry.* Tavistock, London.

Thompson, H. and Thompson, J. (1987), 'Support Groups', in A. Campbell (ed.), *A Dictionary of Pastoral Care.* SPCK, London.

Thwaite, A. (1963), 'Sick Child', *The Owl in the Tree.* OUP, Oxford.

Williams, A. (1985), 'The Value of QALY's', *Health and Social Services Journal*, 94, pp. 3—5.

Wilson, M. (1966), *The Church is Healing.* SCM Press, London.

Wilson, M. (1971), *The Hospital—A Place of Truth.* University of Birmingham.

Wilson, M. (1975), *Health Is for People*. Darton, Longman and Todd, London.

Wilson, M. (1983), *Explorations in Health and Salvation: A Selection of Papers by Bob Lambourne*. University of Birmingham.

Winnicott, D. W. (1964), *The Child, the Family and the Outside World*. Penguin, Harmondsworth.

Wright, F. (1985), *The Pastoral Nature of Healing*. SCM Press, London.

Zola, I. K. (1973), 'Pathways to the Doctor—from Person to Patient', *Social Science and Medicine*, 7, pp. 677—89.

Index